© 2021 Nathan A. Hansen

Nathan A. Hansen
Unintentional Librarian: A Beginner's Guide to Working in a Public Library

All rights reserved. No part of this publication may be reproduced, stored in a retrieval system or transmitted in any form or by any means, electronic, mechanical, photocopying, recording or otherwise without the prior permission of the publisher or in accordance with the provisions of the Copyright, Designs and Patents Act 1988 or under the terms of any license permitting limited copying issued by the copyright holder.

Published by: Scipionic Circle LLC
          Post Falls, Idaho
Library of Congress Control Number: 2021915023

ISBN-13: 978-1-7376309-0-6

Nathan A. Hansen
**UNINTENTIONAL LIBRARIAN:
A BEGINNER'S GUIDE TO WORKING
IN A PUBLIC LIBRARY**

Scipionic Circle LLC

UNINTENTIONAL LIBRARIAN

A BEGINNER'S GUIDE TO WORKING IN A PUBLIC LIBRARY

NATHAN A. HANSEN

For my amazing past, present, and future coworkers.

Contents

Introduction — 1

Chapter One: Service and Patrons — 5

Chapter Two: Technology — 27

Chapter Three: Programming — 35

Chapter Four: Reader Advisory — 47

Chapter Five: Searching — 57

Chapter Six: Community Connection — 65

Chapter Seven: Privacy — 71

Chapter Eight: Collection Management — 79

Chapter Nine: Item Repair — 97

Chapter Ten: Other Stuff — 105

Chapter Eleven: Outlook — 115

Appendix — 123

Introduction

This book isn't intended to be an instruction manual on how to run a public library. It isn't a substitute for learning the nuances that completing a Master of Library and Information Science degree or years of experience can provide. It is a ten-thousand-foot overview for those who, like me, find themselves, or even aspire to be, an unintentional librarian.

Let's start things off on the right foot. There is a difference between a Librarian, with a capital "L," and a librarian, lowercase. The former is a professional who has completed a Master of Library Science or Master of Library and Information Science degree and works in a library. The latter is what the general public titles anyone working in a library. If you work in a library, to them, you're a librarian. For example, I've worked as a circulation specialist, a circulation supervisor, and now an information specialist for a public library district. I don't hold a master's degree in anything. The majority of the public doesn't recognize the difference between those positions and a capital "L" librarian. This is not a phenomenon that exists only in the United States. I've traveled to China and Mexico since working for my library, and people in those countries generally associate working in a library with being a librarian too.

You don't usually need a Master of Library and Information Science to work in a public library or in many cases a library at all. In fact, the head librarian for the Library of Congress isn't required to have one, and the person holding that position didn't have one until Carla Hayden became the head librarian in 2016. That's two hundred and fourteen years after the first Head Librarian for the Library of Congress was appointed to the position and one hundred and twenty-nine years after the first library school was established. I don't know about you, but that is much later than I would have thought.

This book focuses on working in a public library. That is often much different from working in academic, school, private, medical, or law libraries, but many things will overlap. A public library usually has a broader demographic of users. Users span socioeconomic strata, race, gender, age, religions, and other labels we tend to assign to larger groups of people. In those other libraries, you may have users spanning a few of those groups, but rarely will you see all of them. For example, a school librarian may have users that span different socioeconomic backgrounds, genders, and even children experiencing homelessness, but they are all going to be within a particular age span that is limited. At a public library, you will deal with the public. All of it. That public represents the community you serve, allowing you to come to a much deeper understanding of that community. You will learn about things you never imagined would happen in your community and interact with segments of your society you may not have even known existed.

This book is separated into chapters based on topics that are big parts of working for a public library. If every new library employee knew the basics of what's contained in this book, they could focus on what makes each public library unique for its community on their first day. You can pick and choose what you are interested in learning more about and dive directly into those or you can read the whole thing cover to cover. Most importantly, you need to take what you've read here, walk the public library you hope to work for looking for how they deal with these topics, and experience it for yourself.

I'm writing from experience on most of these topics and when I'm not I will tell you and pull from experts who have the experience.

One key thing to remember is that there are a lot of ways to have a public library meet the goals of serving its public. The information you find between these covers is designed to give you a ten-thousand-foot view. That view isn't the only one that matters. Each library will tackle the processes, daily procedures, and solutions to specific problems in the way they feel best fits their community. This book is not the answer to everything you may encounter working in a public library, it is merely a look at what I have seen in practice so you can have an idea of what you MAY experience if you begin working in a public library.

I'll also cover the occupational outlook for library work and get into some of the reasons why I haven't pursued a Master of Library and Information Science degree later in the book. While I don't want to discourage those who want to work toward a Master of Library and Information Science, or discount those who already have one, I will explore the reasons behind my personal decision not to and some reasons why you might consider putting in the work and expense to earn one yourself. Your decision should be yours. While my decision works for me, it may not be the right one for you.

You may be curious as to how I came to work in a public library. It was truly unintentional. You didn't pick up this book for me to bore you with my resume, but I took the circuitous route to find myself in the library. I started out in the landscaping industry, made my way into big-box specialty retail, where I worked as an operations and administrative manager, and wound up as a general contractor before branching into library work in 2016. Before coming to the library, I led teams ranging in number from three to nearly two hundred and formed a myriad of really great connections in my community, connections that only grew in my roles working for the library.

I love working for the public library. I get to help dozens of people each day in meaningful ways. I help them learn about topics they are interested in or need to know; I help grandmas learn how to use the iPad their granddaughter gifted them for Christmas; I help the person experiencing homelessness to have a sense of normalcy in their life; help people find and prepare for their dream career, or just the job they need; and so much more. Helping my community through working at the public library is the most fulfilling thing I have done in my career. If by the end of this book you decide you want to take that journey too, I hope you will find working for a public library as engaging, dynamic, and vital to the health of your community as I do.

Now, let the learning begin!

CHAPTER ONE

Service and Patrons

Having a service mindset is critical to becoming a public librarian. Public libraries exist to serve the needs of the members of the communities in which they reside. That includes all members of those communities, even those who exist on the fringes. If you are the type of person who romanticizes working in a library into someone who gets to stand at a checkout counter, read their book, shush people, and occasionally work a stamp with a due date or help someone find a book, you're in for a little bit of an awakening. Working in a public library, in my experience, looks nothing like that romanticized version. In reality, public libraries are dynamic places where you are going to be pulled by patrons in half a dozen directions at the same time.

If you were hoping to be able to park yourself out of the way and avoid people, working in a public library isn't going to be the job for you. If you were looking to have a big impact on the everyday lives of the people in your community through hands-on interactions that can leave you feeling like you've made a difference, working in a library could be just what you were looking for.

All that being said, there's some romance too. I'm usually the first one in the library every morning. I print the list of holds that patrons placed for items overnight, grab a cart, and head out into the stacks to get them pulled for use. This is the only time of day when the library is truly quiet. You can feel the weight of the books and other materials that sit on the shelves in the silence. With the flick of each light switch, the library slowly reveals itself and whispers of its secrets. Each morning I fall in love with it all over again. Not in love with the place, or the idea, but with the potential it holds and the fact that I'm a part of it.

As you go through your day working in a public library, you have to realize that everything you do, from covering and shelving books to children's story times, is done for the benefit of the patrons. If you approach everything you do with that in mind, you will find even the most menial tasks fundamentally fulfilling. For some people, operating with that mindset can be difficult, but being service-oriented is something that can be learned if you don't already possess it.

As you begin to interact with patrons in the library, you will come across interesting scenarios that will present unique challenges. There is rarely a dull day. I'm going to share with you one of the core beliefs I held when I worked as a retail operations manager; always err on the side of service. This belief served me well in that career and it's served me even better in the library world. If you think about it, in retail there is overhead to manage, sales to focus on, employees who have needs that need to be addressed, and a bottom line that always needs to be considered. A library isn't much different. The one big thing that stands out as a difference is that instead of having someone pay for an item or a service, the library is free. That is a liberating feeling.

There is no ulterior motive. You aren't working to drive up the stock price. You aren't thinking about a bonus check or commission with each and every item that makes its way out of the door. You're not calculating how much more payroll you can add based on sales data. It's wholesome. It's honest. It's true. That's why I love it so much.

To say you won't experience difficulties with patrons as you go through your day would be a false claim. Just like everything else, challenges present themselves and drama appears even when you don't seek it. I like to think of it from the perspective of the Pareto Principle, better known in the business world as the 80/20 rule. Eighty percent of your challenges are going to come from twenty percent of your patrons. You will quickly learn who those twenty percent are. Once you know who they are, you can work toward addressing the root cause of any flawed interactions to make them more pleasant for you and for the patron.

I like to think people don't wake up in the morning saying, "I'm going to be difficult today." That assumption allows me to begin to figure out what is causing the person in front of me to be considered "difficult." Often, once you figure out the cause, you can begin to build a relationship with the person that will be based around more positive interactions.

The following are real-life examples of this theory in action while providing patron anonymity.

Let's call the first person Jane, as in Jane Doe.

When I started working for the library, Jane already had a long-running relationship with the employees of the library. They all knew Jane. They all dreaded her calling on the phone, or worse yet, coming into the library. This is a situation that is antithetical to what the library is supposed to be about. After a few weeks of working at the library, I had my initiation of interacting with Jane. Let's just say it didn't go well. She viciously lashed out at me and said, "You're a moron. How did you even get a job here?" Having worked in retail and dealt with problems that made it through four levels of interaction before they reached me, that was hardly the worst thing that has ever been said to me. I was also fairly confident that I wasn't a moron, a buffoon maybe, but not a moron. My coworkers, some of whom had been working in libraries for decades, found Jane's words particularly grotesque.

Lashing out like this was not uncommon behavior from Jane when working with library employees. In fact, her account had been peppered with notes from libraries across our district documenting their warnings to her. They communicated, in detail, the way she interacted with staff and how they considered it inappropriate and unacceptable. Nowhere in those notes was any indication that anyone had taken the extra step to do the most basic thing from a selling or relationship-building standpoint, build a rapport with her. That doesn't mean people hadn't tried, it just wasn't documented for me to know about. If you, like me, believed the notes that were in her profile, it appeared as though we were relying on the institution we worked for to provide that for us—which can be an unintentional workaround directed at simple problems. You can be an unintentional librarian, but you shouldn't have an unintentional service mindset.

Directly after that interaction, and after listening to everyone else's history of interactions with Jane, I made it my goal to make her experience more pleasant. I started on our very next interaction by listening intently and even taking a few notes so I made sure I had everything—Jane tended to ramble off all her needs in a long string very quickly and expect you to remember it all. I like to think she appreciated the undivided attention that I was giving her and the fact that I was making an effort to ensure I had everything down, even though to this day she hasn't said so. Interaction after interaction, things gradually got better. She started coming in with fewer demands and started slowing the interactions down. One day, she called to get some books with pictures of animals she was embroidering. I asked when she would be coming down for them and she said she would be on her way. I let her know I would need fifteen minutes to sort through what we had and get her the best things for her purpose and she agreed to meet me after that.

When Jane came in, I had pulled pictures from the easy reader, juvenile, and adult sections; flagged the pages that had the best photos; and had everything ready on the counter for her. She ate up that level of service. I stood with her and flipped to the pages in the different books I had flagged so she could see what was there and told her about my passing interest in textile arts, talked about how my mom crocheted and taught me, and had a civil conversation about something she was interested in. I let my curiosity take the lead, positioned her as the expert, and listened to what she had to say. I told her I would love to see her final project when she finished it—and I genuinely did. She has brought in every project for me to look at when she finishes it since, and she always asks to deal with me when she calls or comes in. She now has pleasant experiences at the library.

Now that you've heard my brief retelling of Jane's interactions, I want to point out a couple of things. First, did you notice that I set the goal to make Jane's interaction more enjoyable? If you believe the notes on her profile, for years, library staff had been trying to make their own experience less aggrieved by giving her warnings, threatening to suspend service to her, and making notations on her account about all the steps they took down that road. Not once was it noted that anyone made the effort to do a thought experiment and trade roles with Jane to see how they might make the interactions better for her. That is a critical step of service-oriented interactions. If someone is having a pleasant interaction, they will likely ensure you are having one as well. Think about it; when was the last time you saw someone getting great service from a waiter or waitress who was intently focused on their needs treat their waiter or waitress poorly? Sure, it happens, but it's rare.

Second, sometimes it takes time to build that rapport. No matter how skilled you are at building rapport, it is tough to overcome years of mistrust that build up from interactions based on the experience of the people on the back side of the counter. If you have to repair damage, you must start slowly and be consistent. It will take interaction after interaction to get that person to the point where they feel comfortable enough to allow themselves to have a pleasant experience. Trust is often freely given, but once lost it becomes hard to earn.

Third, I made it a point to always be genuine. I don't have the same reading interests as Jane, who reads several books a month in genres that I have no desire to read. Therefore, the pivotal moment in how she experiences the library was never going to come from me trying to connect with her about what she was reading. That would be disingenuous. Instead, I had to wait for my moment. I had to be patient and trust that the small interactions I was having with her were taking her to a place where she would be comfortable in trusting that she could, in fact, have a pleasant experience in the library. That pivotal moment arrived when she had a project that was something we could relate to together.

Finally, I want to talk about how fragile that trust can be. To this day, years after that interaction brought Jane through to the side of having satisfying experiences at the library, it remains tenuous. Many of my coworkers, some of whom didn't work at the library at the time of Jane's transition, have visible frustration on their faces when she calls and asks for me and if I'm not available she won't let them help her. As fragile as that trust is, Jane is slowly branching out. There is now another library employee who she will also deal with. My hunch is that Jane doesn't want to lose the trust she now has in the library and she is very careful with whom she deals with based on past experiences.

Jane is one example of a type of patron who is going to make up part of the twenty percent who cause eighty percent of challenging patron interactions. She represents the patron who has lost trust in the people representing the institution.

Let's explore another couple of examples; I'll call the first one Karen.

Karen is a regular library patron. I first met her as she was checking out books. She also attends many of our library programs—especially the craft ones. I started having more meaningful interactions with Karen after she attended a writer's workshop series that I put together. She was working on a biography of her parents who fled Europe in World War II. She found my series very helpful in making what she had already written better. But that isn't why we're talking about

Karen. Karen is a complainer. The kids are too loud. The librarian helping that patron with the computer is too loud. Someone is talking on their cell phone. Karen is one of those people who has a romantic ideal of a library. She is someone who thinks the library should be a quiet space; librarians should be ladies with their hair in a bun who wear reading glasses, have their shushing fingers at the ready, and they should only look up from what they are reading to stamp your book. She also takes the position that the library should only be used by those doing serious research. All her expectations align with what the contemporary public library isn't. If Karen didn't bring her complaints to us, as library employees, she would directly engage the offending patron, sparking a conflict.

Kevin is also a complainer. Kevin complains when people are typing on the keyboard too loudly or when teens are using the computers to play video games. The most egregious complaint I've had from Kevin was when, standing in the middle of a full computer lab, he declared, "That black kid stole my phone!" This one is particularly dicey because of the demographics of the library system where I work, which consists of a population that is over ninety-four percent white. Our region also has the unfortunate distinction of being the old home of the Aryan Nations, a white supremacist group from the 1990s, which adds another layer to any confrontations that have racial undertones.

When the Covid-19 pandemic caused new requirements for patrons to be able to use the library, like wearing a face mask, both Karen and Kevin complained. Karen complained that she couldn't hear anyone while they were wearing a mask—even though she seemed to have super-sensitive hearing before the pandemic. Kevin complained that people weren't wearing their mask properly and then promptly pulled his down exposing his nose while he was in the computer lab, nullifying any benefit of protection for him or others that it may have provided. There are people out there who just look for things to complain about. Karen and Kevin seem to be those types of people. So, how do you ensure those people have a pleasant experience at the library while protecting the experience other users are entitled to have?

One of my coworkers had a brilliant solution to gain some social capital with Karen. No matter how much we seemed to pull Karen aside and explain that our public library, at the instruction of our board of directors, serves as an institution to bring the community together and not just a place where a few people sit around reading books for research, she just wasn't getting it. I don't know if it was willful obstinacy that was preventing her understanding or if it was unintentional, but she just couldn't bring herself to comprehend that the role of the public library has shifted over the years. One more thing you need to know about Karen is she taught painting classes at the local community college before retirement. My coworker's brilliant solution was to bring her in as an instructor for a series of painting programs at the library. Karen was honored to be asked and we saw a dramatic decline in the number of complaints she was bringing to us. Additionally, having her teach a program at the library provided us more leverage to use against her directly engaging other patrons about what she thought they were doing wrong. We could take Karen aside and remind her that as someone who is instructing classes at the library, she has become an advocate for the library and in many people's eyes can even represent what the institution is. Since she is now in that position, she needs to be more cognizant about how she interacts with other patrons. If she sees something that needs to be addressed while using the library, she should come to one of the library employees and let them handle it. This message is one she understood.

Kevin had a slightly different solution. You see, Kevin has no desire to be involved with the library. He just wants to come in (every day), work on what he has to on the computer, pick up the items he prints out, and then leave. Anything that disturbs his experience warrants a complaint. The regular complaints about people typing too loud, kids playing games on the computers (Kevin is on the upper end of the age spectrum), and facemask wearing are addressed easily enough with a simple conversation—even though we usually have to have them multiple times. Kevin is also prone to involving the director with his complaints, so the front-line staff tries to intervene before he feels compelled to do so. But he will usually do it anyway. We are fortunate enough to have an experienced director with over forty years of experience who supports the staff, but not all libraries have that luxury. When it comes to dealing with accusations of theft, and the racist tone he took in communicating his concerns, I handled that differently.

If you encounter a situation where two patrons are in conflict, the first thing you should try to do is separate them. I asked Kevin to meet me at the circulation desk so we could address his problem. Once he left, I apologized to the young man who was sitting in the computer lab, let him know I would address the issue, and asked if he wouldn't mind staying until I had made sure I addressed the situation with Kevin. He said he had just started playing his game so he would be around for a while anyway.

When I met Kevin at the circulation desk, I asked him what happened and listened—just listened. When trying to resolve conflicts, we often tend to cut people off before they are done speaking. I catch myself doing that if I don't focus on being present to hear what the person has to say. We just want to get to the bottom of the conflict and get it solved as quickly as possible. That's human nature. However, if we wait the additional fifteen seconds it takes for a person to finish what they are saying, we not only gain social capital with the person, but they usually have the solution tucked somewhere into that last fifteen seconds. It was that way with Kevin. In the last fifteen seconds, he said he set his phone down on the computer desk and that the young man (not the words he used) must have come over and taken it. For the young man in question to have done that, he would have had to get up from his computer and walk eight feet to accomplish the heist. I asked Kevin if he would mind waiting while I went and checked our cameras to see if that was actually what happened. He agreed.

So, off I went to check the camera system. Many libraries don't have CCTV, some in my library district don't, but we are a large enough library with enough issues of concern happening that we do—for better or worse (see chapter seven on library privacy). I reviewed the footage. I watched Kevin come in—he never took his phone out and he never set it on the computer desk. Strike one. I watched the young man come in—he went all the way around the computer lab to get to his computer and never came within eight feet of Kevin's station. Strike two. I watched as Kevin frantically searched his pockets, looked around his station, stood up, and began his accusations. Strike three. I exited the back room to talk with Kevin again.

Now, I think Kevin truly believed his phone had been stolen. What concerns me is our computer lab is full of patrons and he happened to single out the only ethnically diverse person in the room—in a very overt manner—a person who wasn't even closest in proximity to Kevin, three other patrons held that distinction. In light of the review, I knew a few more things and was able to speak with Kevin from a more informed position. I let him know that, from what I could see on the camera, he never took his phone out of his pocket or put it on the computer desk. I also let him know that the patron he accused of stealing his phone didn't come within eight feet of him. I then asked if he could describe the phone so that if it turned up we would know it was his and asked if there was someone we could call if it did. Then came the tough bit. I had to let Kevin know that if he had a concern regarding another patron, he should come and get a member of staff involved. I let him know everyone has the right to expect to have a pleasant experience in our library and that his outburst in the middle of a packed computer lab, dolling out accusations, was not conducive to that expectation and could have been handled much differently. Kevin, who was visibly flustered, turned and stormed out of the library—not my desired outcome. I had hoped he would offer up an apology to the young man. I thought to myself, *I could have handled that better.* Then I went and let the young man know the situation had been addressed, apologized for the negative experience he encountered, and went about my day.

Kevin didn't visit the library for several weeks. When he returned, he sought me out and apologized. Apparently, he had left his phone in his car that day. The fact that he found it when he returned to his vehicle caused him so much embarrassment that he didn't return to the library until he had a chance to reconcile that with himself. Since the episode, Kevin has been much more amenable to letting staff deal with issues, and visits to the director have slowed down even though his regular visits have resumed.

There will be times when you don't get everything correct when it comes to your interactions. Perhaps I could have engaged with Kevin differently and that would have caused him to offer an apology to the young man. Looking back on the situation now, I recognize that there was a slim possibility of that happening to begin with. Ultimately, Kevin wasn't embarrassed about the way he interacted with his fellow patron; he was embarrassed that he forgot he didn't bring in his phone. He may not have even been aware of the racist undertones his outburst contained. It took him weeks to reconcile his embarrassment with himself, and I doubt he ever considered the experience of the young man.

Sometimes we have to allow ourselves the opportunity to learn from our experiences after reflecting on them. There is rarely a one-size-fits-all solution. Gaining experiences and reflecting on them will make it so you are more likely to form positive interactions out of difficult situations. Ultimately, Kevin didn't begrudge me for addressing the issues he portrayed—he still speaks with me and we are on cordial terms—and I had the opportunity to think about how I may interact with someone who puts me, and other patrons, in that situation again.

Not all your issues will happen with regular patrons. Many times they happen with patrons who just happened to need one of the library's services that day. Let's talk about Carl.

I first heard Carl giving someone on our circulation staff a hard time about something; I really couldn't hear exactly what it was about from where I was working, but I could hear the tone of the conversation and it held plenty of tension. I generally try to allow my coworkers the opportunity to handle confrontational situations by themselves and only intervene if asked or if it seems things are getting really out of hand. Those situations, after all, are great ways to learn and hone your service skills. Neither scenario was happening, so I just kept my attention on listening for a shift in the tone, which never came. The next thing I knew, my coworker popped their head in the back room and said that the patron was going after another employee about his issue. That's when I stepped in.

When I went up to Carl, he was struggling to communicate in a manner that many would deem library appropriate. Many curse words and insults were being thrown around by him as I approached. When you approach someone who is in that state, it is important to approach them with a visible sense of authority. While exhibiting that authority, ensure your body language is also nonthreatening. They should know you are someone who will take charge of a situation and do so fairly, respectfully, and with good intentions. You also need to use caution. Make sure you leave their path to the exit door clear. You never know exactly what another person is going to do and people get even more unpredictable when they are under stress, which Carl obviously was. I saw his eyes shift from the employee he was verbally accosting to me and as I approached with my hands up, palms out and open, I said, "Whoa, hold on a minute. You can't communicate to our staff like that."

He looked visibly stunned like he didn't expect someone who worked at a library to actively challenge his confrontation. I continued, "If you would like to tell me what's going on, I'd be happy to see what I can do for you."

A string of expletives came from his mouth; then I encouraged him to take a step over to the edge of the room so we could discuss what was going on out of the way of other people who were trying to use the library. He moved over to the edge, which signaled to me he did want help. I never stepped between him and the exit, which was right behind him. If he felt threatened, he had the option of leaving unobstructed.

I listened to how he viewed the issue. From his standpoint, every time he had ever come to the library to print something out from his Gmail account, the library kept blocking him from gaining access. He had to print something out for a new job he was starting the next day, after being unemployed for over six months, and he didn't want to look like he couldn't even print out a stupid email on his first day.

I reassured him that it wasn't likely an issue with the library, as dozens of people access their Gmail accounts in our library every day, and that if he was willing I could join him and see if we could get him what he needed. He agreed and followed me back to the computer lab.

Once there, I noticed he hadn't logged out of the computer, so it was still sitting on the login screen where he left it. He gave me his email address and as I went to enter it I noticed the caps lock on the keyboard was on. I shut it off and continued. Then he told me his password. I asked him if it was all capitalized (since the caps lock had been on) and he said, "No, just the first letter." I entered his password and got him in.

He was elated.

I then let him know it was a simple mistake that happens pretty often and explained exactly how the caps lock key works, which he wasn't aware of, and told him next time to just be sure to double-check it when he went to enter his password.

Simple fix.

I printed his email for him, got it off the printer and it was high-fives and hugs to everyone on his way out the door (which seemed inappropriate on the opposite end of the spectrum).

Carl is an example of someone who hits a hurdle in what they are trying to do and, because of what is going on in his life, that hurdle gets amplified to be an insurmountable wall. Unfortunately, his frustration was initially viewed by our staff as a threat because of the way he was communicating, and reasonably so. But if you meet frustration as a threat, you aren't going to be likely to offer assistance or help someone overcome an obstacle. Remember, people have stuff going on in their lives we aren't always aware of. Taking the time to really listen to what they believe the issue is can be helpful to you in assessing the situation and coming to a solution.

While I've illustrated a few specific scenarios that you will likely encounter, I have enough to fill an entire book, and you likely will too after a few years working in a public library. I'm not able to cover all the scenarios I've encountered here, but something I can do is clue you in on some other types of patrons that may frequent your library in an effort to, at the very least, help you to think about how you may frame your interactions with them to ensure they are having a pleasant experience.

People experiencing homelessness often frequent public libraries, particularly when the weather is poor. In fact, that's how I returned to the library as an adult. I was living in my truck, working eight hours away from my family and the house I owned for over four months before a transfer for my job went through. Not staying where I was would have been career suicide, so leaving before the transfer wasn't an option. At the time I couldn't afford to pay for the house where my family was living and a place for me to stay where I was, so I lived in the back of my pickup sleeping in a sleeping bag under a blue tarp strung over my pickup rack. I relied on the library for a place to stay informed, entertained, and warm. I also had a monthly gym membership to get a daily workout and shower, but the gym scene really isn't my style. It was in the stacks of the McMinnville Library where I found the works of Epictetus, Marcus Aurelius, Kant, Aquinas, Kierkegaard, Descartes, Voltaire, and even Sartre, which prompted me to go back to school to study philosophy and eventually English and creative writing.

Chances are that you know someone experiencing homelessness and aren't even aware of it. When I was experiencing homelessness, I woke up every day, went to the gym to get a workout in, took a shower, shaved, put on my slacks, dress shirt and tie, and went off to work my salaried job. Most people experiencing homelessness aren't there by choice, they are there through circumstance.

I work at a library in a region where it gets hot in the summer and the winters can be downright frigid. If you were to drive through town you wouldn't think we have very many people experiencing homelessness, but the fact is there are many more than people realize and they span all ages, races, backgrounds, and gender identities. It is important to remember that for most people experiencing homelessness the experience is relatively short-lived. These are individuals and families who will be housed in your community in a few months or weeks and they will continue using your services. The services they access at the library are often the very services that help them find gainful employment and housing.

Another thing to keep in mind is that when your most very basic needs aren't being met, there is little else you can focus on. If you have a person experiencing homelessness who has literally come into your library out of the cold, they haven't eaten for a whole day and just spent the night trying to get some sleep on the bench in the park (or the back of their pickup truck), they aren't going to be receptive to receiving instructions right away. Their interactions with you, and with other patrons, will likely be affected by the fact that they are struggling to fulfill their most basic needs. The lack of quality in their interactions often leads to conflict with others—staff and other patrons alike. Your library likely has a code of conduct that must be followed by all patrons, but it is going to be difficult for some of these individuals to look past their immediate needs to adhere to a code they may view as arbitrary at that moment. My best advice, speak to those who work in your library about how they address patrons with these unique concerns. There are also really great training programs available online you can engage with that will address the specific issues library employees may encounter with the population of people experiencing homelessness.

Teens can be another group that can be more challenging to deal with in a library, particularly when they are in large groups. My library exists within walking distance of two middle schools and two high schools. The number of teens in the building in the afternoons has exceeded over one hundred occasionally and over fifty regularly. Individually speaking, the members of this group can be among the most caring, interesting, funny, and engaged patrons you may experience. However, when members of this age demographic congregate in larger groups, they tend to forget (or more accurately become hyper-aware of) who they are. They begin posturing to impress each other (boys, girls, and those who have alternative gender identities—I've seen them all do it) and that can lead to conflicts on every imaginable level. We have had everything from general verbal disagreements to fist fights and even a teen who brought a gun into the library because he felt "dissed" by one of his peers. Yes, things can escalate quickly.

Similar to the population who is experiencing homelessness, teens may have a difficult time focusing on things outside of their immediate need. Their brains are developing from a child's brain into an adult one and, frankly, that doesn't happen overnight. Now, I'm not suggesting you accept that as an excuse for poor behavior, I am pointing it out so that you are aware that there are often limitations that are physiologically based, not just behavioral choices.

Honestly, I haven't come across a library that has issues with teens (and not every library will have issues with teens) where everything is one hundred percent dialed in. Those who struggle are often continually assessing how they are addressing points of conflict with this demographic. What seems to work well, in general, is to set some reasonable boundaries (if they aren't reasonable, they will never be followed), make sure everyone knows what those boundaries are (having them posted for teens to read is important), formulate consequences, and hold offenders accountable. Consistency is the key with this demographic. If you aren't consistent, then in their eyes you are unpredictable and, therefore, unfair.

Young kids may also become an issue. Libraries are viewed by parents as safe spaces (and they also frequently double as part of the National Safe Place Network). That is an extremely good thing. However, some will take more liberty about allowing their children to "run free," unattended, in the library. We have had children as young as five left without a parent or guardian supervision at the library. We've also had parents dump their toddlers off in the children's section so they can visit the computer lab. Your library likely has something in their code of conduct regarding young children in the library, but when a child is left at the library, it can be a very difficult situation to navigate. First, although we may be parents in our personal lives, we are not the parents of every child at the library. Stepping in as one may put you in a position that you don't want to be in. Second, children have varying levels of confidence, ability, and independence. I have dealt with six-year-olds that were more comfortable and capable of being by themselves at the library than some seventeen-year-olds. I don't know about you, but I don't want to be the person who makes that child lose that level of confidence or capability. How you interact with the child does matter and make a difference. Finally, involve other professionals if needed. Follow your library's policy here, but never feel like you can't involve other trusted members in the community to ensure the child is safe. Those individuals may be another library employee, the child's teacher (the child usually knows their school and teacher's name), law enforcement, firefighters, or social workers. These individuals may be able to help you get in touch with the child's parents or at the very least be a second person to wait with you for the guardian to arrive. When you encounter those parents, make sure you cover with them your library's policy so they understand it. They may just not realize that the library is different from a daycare. If you keep having the same issues with the same individuals, make sure you involve your library's leadership.

Individuals under the influence of alcohol or drugs are, unfortunately, also a common issue with public libraries. Some public libraries have had to go so far as to lock their restrooms or put in special lights to hinder intravenous drug use in the bathrooms. In areas where the opioid epidemic hit particularly hard, many public libraries now have NARCAN (naloxone) in their first aid kits and employees receive training on how to administer it. Your library likely has a policy and procedure in place for dealing with individuals under the influence of substances and substance use in the library as well. That policy is usually based on protecting you and other patrons who are in the library. From personal experience, you can't reason with unreasonable people. Those who are under the influence of substances are almost always unreasonable. Many libraries' policies include contacting law enforcement; however, in my library district, we have libraries that would have to wait half an hour or more for law enforcement to arrive. If that is the case at your library, keep in mind you should never engage a person under the influence of substances alone. Bring another library employee or a patron you know and trust if there is no other option. Sometimes fire departments can respond to calls for assistance in more rural locations much quicker than law enforcement as well. Talk with your library's administration and learn what the options are for your particular library and always err on the side of safety.

CHAPTER TWO

Technology

Every January your library will be flooded with people who just received the latest devices gifted by well-intentioned family members. Those people, who often have no clue how to use their new device, will come to you for help in setting them up, downloading apps, connecting to the internet, Facetiming their grandkids, and any number of other technological miracles that are now newly at their disposal. For a few weeks, every year, the library becomes the Apple bar, Verizon store, Geek Squad, and help desk for the members of your community.

It's yet another amazing thing libraries do for their patrons!

Technology is ever-evolving. Remember that the book itself was once cutting-edge technology that grasped the imagination of everyone who encountered one and put them into a state of awe (something that for some of us has never gone away). Librarians, since their inception, have always been at the forefront of helping people to engage with the new and wondrous technologies of the world. Laozi was a librarian who preserved the wisdom of the warring states period in China through the written word on strips of bamboo. Eratosthenes, the chief librarian of the Library of Alexandria, developed the system of latitude and longitude that we still use to navigate the globe today. Leibniz developed calculus—to every English major's chagrin, myself included. Those are just three broad examples of librarians who directly shaped technologies that we may take for granted today. There are many more. When you work for a library, you join that very lineage, only now the forefront of technology is computers, 3D printers, virtual reality, CNC machines, robotics, and so much more.

As nice as it would be to specialize in one thing, the reality is that when you are helping the public, people are going to come in with questions that fit their specific needs. You will have to know, or at least learn, how to download your library's eBook lending software onto an Amazon Kindle along with an iPhone and any other device that is out there or happens to come along. Knowing one but not the others just isn't going to be sufficient because your patrons will have different devices. Keeping up to date with the newest tech items as they come out is a huge challenge. Digital technologies, in particular, change at an exponential rate. If you're lucky, your library has planned for this and brings in new devices for you to experience, learn, and become adept at using to ensure you can help patrons with different devices. Even if the library brings in new items for you to experience, they won't be able to bring in everything for you, so you'll have to learn beyond what you can experience.

The best place to turn to learn about new technologies, and how to use them, is online. Libraries, public libraries in particular, usually lag behind that early-adopter status. That means by the time something comes into the mainstream, where you may have to deal with it, there is usually a trove of blogs full of how-to articles and YouTube videos explaining how the device operates. Nine times out of ten, once you learn the basics of how an operating system works, you will look like a rock star to the person coming in to get help setting up their new device. So, that's my advice ... learn the basics of the different operating systems. Learn Windows, Android, and IOS operating systems first because that will be the vast majority of what you will be dealing with. You likely have a phone in your pocket and a computer in your home that uses these already, so learning the odd one out shouldn't be too daunting. Learning the Microsoft Office suite is also really helpful, but with the rise of Google many people, particularly those who are of younger generations, are switching over to using the free Google Workspace as well, so learn that too.

Most people coming in to use a computer have really basic questions. How do I save a file? How do I open a file? Where did my document go? How do I use the spellchecker? What is the cloud? How do I access my email? How do I print this? How do I attach my resume to this job application? Can you show me how to get on Facebook? How can I scan a document? All these questions may seem easy to you if you've grown up using computers, but you will encounter a significant portion of the population who haven't had the experience of interacting with these things when you work at the library. If you can't answer those ten questions, that's okay, but do yourself a favor and learn how to do those things before you have a bunch of patrons asking you to fix their problems. Pop onto YouTube, or just ask another library employee (that's part of why they are there, to help people learn new technologies or technologies they haven't been exposed to, they won't hold it against you).

Many libraries have access to online computer training. My library subscribes to a service called Learning Express that offers in-depth training on the entire Microsoft Office suite, Adobe Illustrator, Adobe Photoshop, and Windows 7, 8, and 10. Individuals looking to learn about these software programs can go through video tutorials, at their own pace, and become proficient. Ask your library if they offer any of these types of resources, and then engage with them yourself so you can direct other patrons to them with confidence.

There is a ton of training that Google has available for their free resources as well. Many businesses are turning to this platform because of the ease of use, the ability for different applications within the Google Workspace to interact with one another, and the ability to easily collaborate and share documents, calendars, forms, and other things with others. These training resources are easy to find. Simply type "Google Workspace Training" in any browser's search function and they will likely be the first thing you see. Some training companies want you to pay for their service, but in my experience, these pieces of training are often a scam, and the free ones Google offers are really well put together and usually all you need.

Once you understand how the three operating systems work (Windows, Android, and IOS), can answer those ten basic questions patrons usually ask, and have gone through training on the Office suite and Google Workspace, you will be able to handle ninety-five percent of what you will encounter from patrons at the library or be able to find the answer. You're ready to start moving into the other aspects of library technology.

Many public libraries have gone beyond basic computer usage—being able to type up a document or spreadsheet and print it out. They are expanding into maker spaces, which may include 3D printers, CNC machines, and laser cutters. These items operate on basic CAD principles. You may not have had experience with Computer Automated Design, otherwise known as CAD, before, but it is hardly considered "new" technology at this point. In fact, many businesses rely on individuals being able to understand a CAD system, that's one reason why many public libraries have started to bring in resources that will allow patrons to experiment with them.

If you've never had experience with a CAD-type system, you can experiment with one for free called "Sketch Up." Some of the basic concepts you should focus on when experimenting with these types of systems are thinking in three dimensions, learning about vector paths and files, and thinking about the output medium. Don't worry, there are lots of Sketch-Up tutorials online, including full-fledged YouTube courses you can engage with for free.

If you've ever taken a drawing class you've experienced thinking about representing a three-dimensional object on a two-dimensional plane. When you build that three-dimensional object in a CAD program, it too is represented on the two-dimensional plane of the computer screen. The difference is in that CAD program, you can rotate that object to view it from any possible direction. Top, you got it. Bottom, you betcha. Left or right side, yep, those too. CAD programs take what used to take multiple drawings to represent and put them into one type of file that can be read and interpreted by something like a 3D printer to make an actual three-dimensional item. Pretty cool.

Vector paths or files are also really interesting. If you've ever tried to enlarge a photograph and encountered it getting fuzzy or pixelated, you've experienced the phenomenon that vector paths and files were designed to fix. A vector path or file can be enlarged or shrunk to whatever sizes you want while maintaining relational accuracy. It doesn't matter if the item you want is the size of a thimble or the size of a school bus. With a vector file, the relation between individual points on the item will remain the same. Many graphic design files are vector files. A vector file can be easily converted to a non-vector file, like a simple image file, but going in the other direction is much more difficult.

Finally, thinking about the output medium is very important. Are you adding material, like a 3D printer does, or are you removing material, like a CNC does? Perhaps you are working two-dimensionally with a laser cutter. The output is important to understand. If you are building up layers of material with a 3D printer, you have to have a layer below for the next layer to adhere to. In other words, you can't put something on top of nothing. Not understanding how this works will lead to a failed print. On the opposite side of the spectrum, a CNC machine takes material away. If it is a top-down removal, you won't be able to undercut something without ruining the layer above. These types of problems foster organizational thinking and problem-solving, which is yet another skill that libraries can help people understand through the use of these tools.

Many libraries are also moving into helping their patrons experience new technological experiences like virtual reality and flying drones. Now, you may think that virtual reality is something really cool for playing video games, and it is, but it goes so much further than that. There are virtual reality programs that can help you explore national parks or step into a Vincent van Gogh painting.

If you are someone with mobility issues who wants to hike the Grand Canyon, you can in virtual reality. If you want to better understand the paint strokes of *Starry Night*, you can get right into the painting, shrink down to the size of an ant and walk across the surface where it looks like frozen waves on the ocean. Virtual reality is also used to help train surgeons, pilots, and bomb technicians. Plus, the video games are amazeballs.

Drones have allowed people to create their own virtual reality tours. I've spoken with photographers who have used them to create virtual reality walk-throughs of homes for realtors, shoot epic footage at the local rock climbing cliffs, and even do tours around a town for the local chamber of commerce. Roofing companies have used them to inspect roofs without setting a foot on them and first responders have used them to search for people and deliver emergency items. Drones are becoming more commonplace and they are another tool that some libraries are adding into their resources for people to experience, even if it's only to get an aerial shot of their house.

For all of the really cool pieces of technology that your library may have, nothing replaces having people on staff who understand their value and can communicate what they are used for, and how to use them, to the public. That's what you get to experience if you work for a public library. The enthusiasm you approach technology with will help to direct the attitude and growth of the people in your community, and what's more fun than that?

CHAPTER THREE

Programming

One of the most rewarding things you can engage in while working for a public library is programming. It doesn't matter if it is for adults or children, whether you are leading the program or supporting it, or if it is a program the library has developed with their own staff or a program the library is hosting an outside presenter for, you will come away from the experience feeling like you've done something amazing for someone in your community. Programming can also add an additional level of stress to your day, week, or even month (depending on how much is involved with your program). I'm going to provide you with some advice based on real-world experiences that will help to mitigate any stress that may come your way as you begin to wade into the waters of library programming.

My experience with running programs started well before I started working for the library. I've served as a Cubmaster and merit badge counselor for the Boy Scouts of America designing and implementing programs to teach valuable skills to boys and young men (I'm happy to see they are letting girls participate now too). I also designed programs for adults when I worked in retail, which covered various building and home maintenance topics for customers, along with training programs for employees. Before all that, I was a frequent presenter for a public radio station covering gardening topics. I've been putting together programs to help people gain valuable skills and information, while having some fun along the way, since I was in high school. Now I have grey in my beard and less hair on my head—oh, so much less hair.

Throughout all of those experiences the one thing I've learned is that no matter how much preparation you do, you are going to be surprised by something. However, the more planning and preparation you do the less likely those surprises are going to derail what you are trying to accomplish. It's great to say, "You need to prepare." It sounds nice and easy, but in reality, you are going to be pulled in several different directions when you work at a public library, and finding time to devote to that process can be a challenge. So, where do you start?

You have to decide what kind of program you are going to put together. The fact that you are going to get pulled in all sorts of directions throughout your day is actually an advantage here. It provides you an opportunity to get involved with all sorts of people in your community. Because of that involvement, you are going to gain a greater understanding of the needs of your community. There are books and librarian blogs out there that can direct you toward different types of programs you might want to try at your library, but nothing is going to be better than listening to those in your community and working toward addressing their needs.

After you recognize what the needs of your community are, you can start coming up with a list of possible programs that can address those needs. For example, if you are helping a lot of people file for unemployment benefits or hone their resumes you might consider some programs that focus on job skills, host a job fair, or organize mock interview workshops. These things would all tie into that need you are seeing in your community.

Sometimes you have to get a little more creative. Maybe you have a group of retirees who visit the library for socialization. But instead of all of them showing up at the same time and socializing with each other, they hang around your circulation desk having conversations with staff members. Maybe those staff members, although very empathetic, feel like they can't get what they need to get accomplished done. Perhaps you could organize a weekly short story book club, or coffee and coloring group, or craft group on weekday afternoons and encourage them to come and participate.

You can also consider seasonal needs. Maybe you organize an afternoon where people can bring apples from their gardens down and have them mashed and pressed to make their own cider. Or maybe you gather a group of kids together to make snow ice cream. You could sponsor a summer reading "beach read" where everyone brings a book to the beach and you provide snacks and refreshments for anyone joining in. Seed starting or sharing events are great for spring too!

Once you understand the need and have a list of ideas, you need to determine the location where you will have the program. Doing programs at the library is a great option. We all want to see those spaces used and inviting people to use the space they help to fund lets them see what their taxes are paying for. But I'm going to let you in on something that very few want to talk about; the people who come to programs at the library are usually people who are already using your library. Don't get me wrong; that is a wonderful thing! However, if one of your goals is to reach new people with your services, you should consider going out into the community and meeting people where they are. Host a trivia night at the bowling alley, take your short story book club to the senior center, and host that cider press in your own booth at the local farmers' market (I bet they will even donate the space, especially if some of their vendors are selling apples) and while you're there have a story time about apples for the kids, the parents will love you for it. You will reach new people and can encourage them to get involved with the library.

So, let's take stock of where we are. We've sought out the need, come up with ideas, and picked a location where we want to have the program. We now have enough of a handle on what is going on to start reaching out for help. That's right, REACH OUT FOR HELP! If you're planning a program that involves other community organizations or locations, you have to reach out early. If we go back to the cider press example, you probably need to be reaching out to the person who has the cider press and the farmers' market three months in advance. That isn't unrealistic because most of those people are looking that far ahead or further. Additionally, even if it is something you are doing in-house, like a book club, it can help to involve some of the patrons who you know would be interested in participating to help pick titles (I would suggest you provide them a list and they pick a few from that list to start with). Maybe one of the patrons who wants to participate in the book club is an awesome baker and wants to make some treats for refreshments (actually, at my library, one of my coworkers started a cookbook book club where everyone picks something from a cookbook and makes it and they have a potluck to taste everything. It is really popular—just another idea you can use). Don't be afraid to ask for volunteers and subject matter experts to get involved, that's a part of community building—which is a primary function of many public libraries.

Once you have your help lined up, you can work with them to figure out the details. What time is it going to start? Who is going to do what? What kind of materials do you need to pull together? How are you going to market and advertise the event? What does success look like? That last one is really important. If you don't have any idea of what success looks like, you don't know how to structure your program for the participants. Remember, you are putting this program on for the members of your community, not just because you want to do that craft project yourself (although that can often be a bonus).

You need to get your materials ordered and on the way. You can look at places like Amazon, Etsy, eBay, and local dollar stores for materials. If you're ordering online, make sure you factor in shipping. If you're using Prime shipping through Amazon, it can be pretty reliable, but if you are ordering through one of their third-party vendors or ordering from Etsy or eBay, you can save a ton of money, but they may be coming from overseas and can take substantially longer in shipping times. Sometimes you can get local businesses to donate materials for your programs. Don't be afraid to ask around and leverage your community connections.

Marketing your event is often the largest challenge. You are putting in a ton of effort to pull together something from nothing and if no one shows, you will feel discouraged and maybe even defeated. That means you need to spend some time thinking about how you are going to get the word out about your program. There are little things you can do that can have a big impact. Something simple as printing out some flyers to post in the library and some bookmarks that you put in books for patrons as they check out can get the attention of your regular patrons. Social media accounts can also be leveraged to reach patrons and let them know what you are doing. The key to leveraging these resources is capturing the patrons' attention, so make sure your visuals are on point and relevant to your topic. You can also leverage community contacts. Reach out to the local newspapers, put up flyers at the local community college, and talk with the people who run the food banks, laundromats, grocery stores, and barber shops and salons to see if you can place your flyers there. You can also leverage other organizations in your community like the Boys and Girls Club, Rotary Club, Chamber of Commerce, and even local government (I've heard of libraries getting programs advertised in residents' utility bills). All of these options, and anything else you can think of, are open to you.

Now that you have some ideas about where you can get the word out, you need to be sure you're thinking of your target audience and make sure your marketing plan keeps them in mind. If your program is targeted to seniors, you aren't going to be marketing it in elementary schools. If your program is for a new teen program, you're likely wasting your time with the Chamber of Commerce, but the Parks and Recreation department might help you out. Spend your time where you will have the biggest impact. Don't forget to start your marketing campaign a few weeks ahead of time and ramp it up a couple of days before your event. People usually need to see whatever you are promoting at least seven times before it even registers as an item of interest for them, so keep that in mind.

I like to reach out to anyone who is involved in the event the week before, just to touch bases with them and make sure everything is still on track. You will likely find everyone is taking their role in the process seriously, but I have had some folks that needed a little extra encouragement. This also allows you to see if there is anything that is falling through the cracks and come up with solutions to address those issues before the day of your event.

In addition to reaching out the week before an event, if your event is dependent on an outside presenter, I recommend you call or email them the day before just to make sure everything is on track. This serves as an opportunity to run down your checklist of things you need to get ready for them as well. If they need an audio setup or the ability to run a PowerPoint, this is the time to make sure you know all that. If they've agreed to be recorded so you can post the event on social media channels it's also a good time to remind them you will have a release for them to sign and remind them they will be on camera so they can make sure they wear something they are comfortable being filmed in. I usually ask if they would like to show up a little early so I can run through any last-minute needs and do sound checks and make sure everything is the way they need it.

When the day of your event arrives, you are going to have a lot to get done. You're going to initiate your last marketing push (if you're planning on that being a social media blast, I recommend scheduling that ahead of time so you don't have to worry about it). Get this done first so you can focus on everything else. Setting up the space you are using is going to take some time. Meeting with your speaker or volunteers is crucial to make sure everyone is ready and has any concerns they may have addressed. Greeting people as they arrive to make them feel welcome and assuage any apprehensions they may have toward a social gathering is also important. Some people are trepidatious and need you to reassure them they are in the right place.

If you have a speaker, make sure you know how to pronounce their name properly (I speak from the experience of having butchered speakers' names before—that's right, more than one). It's also a good idea to go over your introduction with them. Over the years I've found many author websites have details wrong, especially if they are authors from larger publishers who slapped together an author site for them quickly. Authors are happy to help correct any issues if you review your introduction with them before the event (this can be done easily over email). Yes, as the host, you need to introduce your speaker. Even if they plan on giving their background as part of their presentation you need to establish the relationship between the library and the speaker. If the speaker is going to go into their own credentials something as simple as, "The (library) is happy to bring you today's speaker on (topic). (Speaker's name) has a wealth of expertise surrounding (topic) that they will discuss as they get into their presentation and it is my pleasure to host them on behalf of (library) for you today. Please join me in welcoming (speaker's name)." Remember to applaud and the audience will generally follow; welcome the speaker on stage with your body language and then graciously fade into the back of the room to welcome latecomers or assist with technical aspects of the presentation.

No matter how much planning goes into a program, there will be times when things blow up in your face. Once I had a speaker for a "Make it Happen" goal-setting program who came down with the flu the day of the presentation. We tried contacting them that morning to confirm and had to leave voicemails. I and my coworker who was helping with the program assumed they were busy but would be there that afternoon for the presentation. The speaker was so ill that calling us to let us know never even occurred to them because they forgot what day it was.

As my coworker and I welcomed patrons to the program, although the speaker still hadn't arrived, I had a mini huddle with my partner and discussed what we should do. After all, the program was named "Make it Happen" and we weren't about to let it not happen. I stood at the front of the audience of fifteen people and apologized that our speaker for that day had something come up and would not be able to make it (at the time I didn't know what that something was or even if the speaker was going to pop in a few minutes later). I asked them to bear with me for a few moments so we could shift gears and present another topic that also discussed the theme. I took the nods in the audience as a sign they were willing to see what we had up our sleeves.

My coworker had just returned from a trip to New Zealand so began talking about some of the hurdles that travel can throw at you while I whipped out the flash drive from my pocket to open a PowerPoint I hadn't quite finished that discussed a month I spent in China studying Taoist philosophy with my sixteen-year-old son. I quickly altered some slides and had a quick presentation pertaining to "Make it Happen" ready and raring to go in the ten minutes my coworker used to set the premise of my talk.

I talked about how I had spent my entire life after high school wanting to visit places and experience cultures around the world and how life often got in the way. School, marriage, career, kids, there always seemed to be something that was more important and more pressing. When I turned thirty-five, I made a decision that I was going to "Make it Happen." That's when I discussed the steps I took to allow my son and me to explore one of the three pillars of thought that serve as the foundation to the culture of China, and do it for an entire month all for less than $5,000.

It turned out to be a great program. I talked with many of the audience members about their travels to Germany, Spain, and South Africa and encouraged them to share some of the challenges they had to overcome and how they did it with the group. It became very interactive and before we knew it, we had blown past our hour-long program and we still had an excited group of people discussing how to get things done. All in all, it was a success.

The point of that story is, even if everything seems to be fine, a last-minute issue can threaten to derail what it is you are doing. Part of working in a public library is being able to respond quickly to the needs of your community. This was just another version of that. By being nimble enough to embrace the moment as an opportunity instead of a disaster, my coworker and I quickly pivoted into something the participants found engaging and useful. We didn't send those fifteen people home disappointed. Instead, we sent them home dreaming about what they might be able to accomplish regardless of the obstacles put in front of them and I received a request from one of the participants to come and speak at another community group's event.

When you talk about giant obstacles, perhaps the largest one I've experienced in putting on programs was the Covid-19 restrictions of 2020. When the pandemic began to sweep across the country, libraries found their buildings shuttered. The thing to keep in mind is the idea of a library is so much more than the building that houses the institution or even the ability to meet in person. The library where I work closed in March of that year; by April I had partnered with our Youth Services Specialist to create dynamic story times to post online. These weren't just the librarian sitting in a chair reading a book (although many libraries did that, and in the context of the pandemic doing anything at all was quite a challenge, so please understand that there is no negativity in that statement). I brought my personal filming equipment into the library and set up a green screen where the children's librarian read their book, sang their songs, and did a full story time. Then I took the book, scanned the illustrations, isolated specific elements, and made an animated story time where the librarian was interacting with the story. The librarian became a part of the storybook. Ten months after posting that first story time, it's been viewed over ten thousand times totaling over four hundred hours of viewing time. We've posted many more with similar results.

If the closures of 2020 taught me anything, it's that programs don't always have to be in-person. While I love in-person programs, and so do many of our patrons, having a story time that an isolated mother, in the middle of a pandemic, can show their child after bath time becomes just another aspect of the library that people can use to enhance their everyday lives.

Eventually, the library purchased filming equipment and we've put together programs for adults, programs that explain the Dewey Decimal System, a teen summer writing series, a series which we partnered with the local museums to discuss aspects of local history, and so many other things that our patrons have engaged with. I can't stress enough that the key to thinking about library programming is to think about how it is filling the needs of your community and keeping the end user in mind. I am not a children's librarian, but there was a need for those kids to hear stories and engage with the children's librarian whom they have come to love through the in-person programs they've attended. I had a skillset that could help facilitate that, so I stepped in to lend a hand. That's what working at a public library is all about, filling the needs of the community; and each employee of the library is going to bring their talents and expertise to help in that goal.

CHAPTER FOUR

Reader Advisory

If your library is anything like the one where I work, you will likely receive dozens of new books each week. When you combine those books with the rows upon rows of books that you likely haven't read, how could you possibly feel adequate enough to be able to recommend the perfect read for a patron? Reader advisory is a part of the job, after all.

We all have our favorite authors, genres, and maybe even publishers that we gravitate toward. That inevitably means we have gaps in what we have read. I work with people who will read a book a day, I average about a book a week (from what I can tell that's pretty close to average for those who work in libraries, we typically have a lot going on), but even those who read a book a day can't cover the number of new books we receive in January throughout a calendar year. You can try to be a cultural omnivore, but is it going to make you happy? Probably not. So, what happens when a patron comes in who likes the exact opposite of what you do, something you would never touch because it just doesn't appeal to you? You can't always rely on someone being on staff that day who will fill your gaps; you're going to have to learn some tricks to make sure that patron gets a good read.

First, let me clarify that I am talking about advisory for videos, music, and other media as well in this discussion. The word "read" is a stand-in for how people engage with all forms of media.

What actually constitutes a good read? From the standpoint of a library employee, a good read is one that the patron is going to engage with and fits their (the patron's) reading goals. If they are looking to learn something, you better make sure you know that. If they are looking to chill out and have a nice relaxing read you need to know that too. You're reading this book because it likely aligns with your goals. I haven't been ambiguous about the title so I hope I'm meeting your expectations. If you don't match the book you recommend to your patron's needs, they likely aren't going to trust you again.

There are a bunch of tools that you can leverage to make sure you are getting a patron a read that fits their needs and desires. But you have to know what those desires are. Here are some examples of questions you can ask:

- What was the last book you read that captivated you and what was it that you found so interesting?
- Who's your favorite author and what do you like about them?
- What is your favorite genre and why?

- Are you looking for something that is similar to what you like or something that is going to take you someplace different?
- Is there a particular topic you want to explore?

Did you notice that I started with questions that are going to get the patron talking? They weren't simple yes or no questions. When they start to open up a little with the questions at the beginning, they will likely expand on their answers by the end to ensure you have a well-rounded understanding of what they are looking for. Your questions don't have to be exactly these, but they should use a similar tactic. Don't start with close-ended questions, those simple questions that have one-word answers. You need to get your patron talking so you can leverage your librarian tools to get them what they actually want. Using this tactic works for fiction and nonfiction, books, music, and movies.

Once you've asked those questions and received your patron's answers, what do you do with that information? If you're lucky enough to work for a library that has access to a resource like NoveList, that's where you're going to go. Most public libraries either have a subscription to NoveList of their own or have one through their state library association, so we're going to cover some cool things that you can do with it first and then move on to some alternatives.

NoveList by EBSCO is a database of books where you can look for things like read-alikes. Let's say the last book that got your patron excited was one they read in high school, *The Great Gatsby*. You can simply type that title in the search bar and up comes the option of either "Title Read-alikes" or "Author Read-alikes"—this is why you ask the questions to find out why they liked what they did, because you need to narrow down if it was the writing style or the type of story that they were most compelled by. The beautiful thing about NoveList is it not only tells you that something is a read-alike but also why it is a read-alike. For example, *Lady Chatterley's Lover* is a "Title Read-alike" because both novels have, "themes centered on the social disruptions of industrialization, women's rising expectations, and the mixing of social classes and the empty lives of the wealthy." On the other hand, John O'Hara is an "Author Read-alike" because he also, "[writes] atmospheric, leisurely paced stories about manners and social class in 1920s and 1930s America. Their haunting stories are elegantly written, psychologically intimate, and filled with melancholy, though John O'Hara's work is often less subtle and more sarcastic than F. Scott Fitzgerald's." As you can see, the succinct descriptions of who, or what, it points you toward are short enough to be read quickly and detailed enough for you to make a great recommendation—if you do your leg work by asking the patron the right questions to begin with.

NoveList is also going to provide you with multiple options, not just one. Both the "Author Read-alike" and the "Title Read-alike" had nine recommendations each. The resource is also going to give you a popularity rating, Lexile and Accelerated Reader ranges, and target audience information. You can get all of this in about a minute, which makes it particularly helpful when you have a line of patrons waiting for your time and attention.

The other cool thing about NoveList is that when you get that patron—and it will happen often—who wants you to find a children's book about, "A bathtub that all these animals try to fit in," you can simply type in "animals in a bathtub" and find *Big Red Tub* by Julia Jarman. There are lots of great tools in NoveList that can help you advise your readers (and tutorials on how to use them on their website), but before I turn this chapter into an infomercial for NoveList, let's move on to alternative options.

Book people—all types—engage in their own forms of social media. You can often find authors on Twitter recommending something that had them particularly inspired, but when it comes to readers, the social media platform they are using—at least for now—is Goodreads. What's great about Goodreads is it is populated by everyday readers, not the literati gatekeepers of the publishing world. Your library also doesn't have to pay for a subscription to use it.

Simply searching a book's title will usually net you some insightful reviews and the great thing is if you find someone who has a particularly insightful review, you can click on their user name to see what is on their favorites shelf. That will usually net you some books that are in line with the book you are looking at. Additionally, many titles will have a section labeled "Readers Also Enjoyed" that is going to have books that are similar in some way to the book you're looking at (this feature does take a certain number of reviews to kick in). You also have the option to click the "Libraries" button to quickly see which libraries have a listing in the WorldCat system (more on that in chapter eight). That's an easy way to quickly see if your library holds the item without having to bounce back and forth between the resource and your catalog.

Goodreads also has their reader awards that you can consult. These are items in all sorts of categories that readers have found particularly awesome! They don't only do fiction either, you can see awards for nonfiction titles as well (something that other websites often overlook).

So, where does the "Social" aspect come in? You can sign up for Goodreads with just an email address or through social media apps or online accounts that you already use (Facebook, Twitter, Google, Amazon, or Apple). Once you've registered your account you can search out your friends—or other public librarians—and add them (if you sign in using a social media account like Facebook, it will prompt you to add your friends from there who already have Goodreads accounts). Then you can set up your basic "Shelves." The default shelves are "Read," "Currently-reading," and "To-read." You can leave reviews of books you've read and read the reviews your friends have left for the books they've read. The book catalog is tied to Amazon's database so pretty much any title is available, with a few exceptions, to be added to a shelf. You can also manually add titles that Amazon doesn't have in its database, so don't fret if what you were looking for isn't there. You can list your favorite authors and in most cases follow them to see what they're reading (assuming they're still alive). There are also social groups you can join. Some of these groups are set up by publishers and others are virtual book clubs. And you can leave comments on your friends' pages. It really does become an online community of book lovers. Best of all, you get to avoid everyone's political, religious, and social opinions that are plastered all over other social media because people on here really do just want to talk about books!

Knowing all that, if your patron wants to sign up for their own Goodreads account, you can often recommend things directly to them; they can review aspects of your recommendation along with reviews, add it to their shelf, and they can pull up their "To-read" shelf when they visit you again to know what they are looking for. You can also start to build additional shelves that you can consult the next time someone comes in looking for a steamy romance when that isn't your thing. Make some shelves for quick reference of common genres and topics and when you hear someone talk about that great book they just read, add it to the corresponding shelf so you can use it as a recommendation.

We've covered two great digital sources you can leverage to help with reader advisory, but there are some old-school email and analog options you should be aware of too. Almost every publisher has a newsletter you can subscribe to that will float right into your inbox. These will often have little blurbs about the book, release dates, and maybe even some pre-launch critic reviews. These newsletters are selling tools for the publisher, so keep that in mind, but there are always some good options for your patrons in them. There are also trade journals and magazines available for you to use as well. One of my favorites is "Booklist." I can always seem to find good articles in there among the troves of new releases that they discuss. You can also keep an eye out on best-seller lists. In my library we photo copy *The New York Times* list each week and set it out for our patrons to look at, many of them appreciate not having to walk back to the newspaper section or search it up online to get the information.

No matter how you choose to keep up to date about what is out there, the key is that you are doing it for your patrons. When they see you are working hard to find them the book that fits their needs and you're not recommending something you liked just because you liked it, they will appreciate your efforts. That goes a long way in how they think and feel about your library, as well as how much they will use it.

One of the key aspects of reader advisory is not just knowing what to recommend but also knowing how to communicate those recommendations. Many people will look at you as a literary expert just because you work at a library. It doesn't matter if you don't know the difference between Foucault and Derrida or Structuralism vs. Postmodernism—they usually don't care—you're the expert. You're behind the desk and they are on the other side of it, so think about the relational position and how that contributes to the way someone views you. Because they have assumptions about your literary authority, your words will carry weight. If you speak down to what they like, you are telling them that what they like is sub-standard, essentially shaming them. You're "yucking their yum" and no one likes a yum-yucker. Just because you don't like Westerns doesn't mean they don't have merit, so don't disparage them because of your personal opinion.

The vocabulary you use in communicating about items to someone also makes a difference. Is the book slow or is it measured? Slow has a negative connotation, measured is more contemplative and intentional so it has a more positive connotation. They mean the same thing as far as the book is concerned, but they are going to make the person hearing about them have a different emotional reaction, and aren't books all about emotional reactions? Similarly, fast-paced isn't very descriptive but an action-packed-thrill-ride that keeps you thirsty until the last page is going to make that patron more aware of what they're in for.

Think about the words you would use to describe different aspects of the media you're recommending. How would you describe the pacing? Is it relaxed, tense, engrossing, measured, blistering, or hurried? How would you classify the way the author developed and presented their characters? Were they realistic, presented from multiple points of view, endearing, familiar, well-rounded, loveable, or quirky? How was the storyline? Was it filled with the soft gentleness of a spring afternoon, packed with "secure the perimeter" action, gory, was it an existential quest, did it pivot around a single character? What was the atmosphere like? Were you sucked into the dark underbelly of noir fiction? Was it as edgy as a razor blade, as romantic as soft kisses, or as fun as puppy slobber? These are all the things you need to communicate when you are talking about a piece of media you are advising on. You'll eventually come up with your own favorite phrases that will put your flair on your advisory. Once you get to that point, it gets far less intimidating.

Remember to let the person you're advising know that these are just titles for them to try on. Some people need your permission that it is okay if they don't power through that four-hundred-page book or two-and-a-half-hour movie just because you said it should be in line with what they like. I like to tell them, "Life's too short for books (or movies) you don't find interesting." Just because one person liked it doesn't mean the next one will and your patrons have to understand that that's okay. A library is like a dressing room, you can try on the pants, but you don't have to make them your favorite pair. They can always return the book. You can even let them know that no one will ever know if they read it. This isn't high school, there are no quizzes along the way or a test at the end. If they put it in the book return, it just goes back to the shelf or on to the next person.

CHAPTER FIVE

Searching

One of the functions you need to know when you are christened into library land is how to search in an actual database. The database subscriptions that libraries (or their state associations) purchase are different from Google and you may have a bit of a learning curve in dealing with them.

First of all, they aren't all exactly user-friendly. Frankly, I don't know why libraries and associations aren't thinking of the end user experience more often with these products. For example, in my state, we have a database system that is paid for by the state's library commission. There are over one hundred and fifty academic research and learning databases available to any resident of the state by just typing in their zip code and the name of their city. It is an amazing resource that is so confusing that the local high school librarian even hesitates to use it. Each new semester I can expect a list of articles the juniors and seniors are trying to find for their projects to show up in my email inbox. Inevitably, I pop into the resource and, seventy percent of the time, the articles are right there. That being said, the resources have been getting more user friendly. Many now have drop-down boxes you can select categories to search within, so don't be afraid to use them.

Now, the school librarian who isn't showing those students how to use a resource like that properly is not really helping them. To be clear, I don't place the blame on the school librarian, they have a ton of kids (the average graduation year in their school has well over three hundred kids and there is only one librarian with all of those kids doing their research in a two-week timeframe), and the resource is clumsy and isn't entirely conducive to the end user having a pleasant experience. The blame, at least the largest share, lies at the feet of whoever designed the resource in the first place. However, the students who don't learn how to use those resources are going to be the adults who are going to need someone to help them through the process of using them in a couple of years when they are researching to form a business plan, trying to understand a medical diagnosis, or working on their college projects. That person who is going to help them, if you're working at a public library, may just be you.

Just because you have access to these databases, which are juggernauts of information, doesn't mean that you are going to use them to answer every question you don't know. The vast majority of the questions you are going to get daily are going to be answered just as easily in Google, or Bing, or Duck Duck Go, or whatever other search engines you prefer to use with your internet browser. They are the questions like what's the phone number for the local animal shelter, what's the population of the next town over, what was the name of the actress in a particular movie, how much is it to rent an apartment in your city, what's the mailing address for the president of the United States so they can send them a letter (if you don't know that one already, you'll likely learn it soon enough). Use your everyday search engine to quickly answer these types of questions for your patrons, that's the beauty of our modern internet. The library databases are for more in-depth answers to questions.

If you have someone trying to find out everything about a medication they are taking, your library probably has access to a medical database that is going to give more accurate information than what a generic search engine is going to turn up. If someone is trying to write an in-depth paper on the history of women's suffrage, they are going to find reliable, vetted information in a library database. If someone is looking up the source material a journalist used to write a particular article so they can assess the interpretations for themselves, they will likely find it through a library database. Genealogical research is often augmented through library databases. These resources are going to go deep and they are far more reliable as good sources of accurate information than the top results on Google. So how do you use them?

To start with, you need to understand Boolean operators. Boolean operators are logical expressions that a computer can interpret to get you the information you need. The three basic ones you need to know are: AND, OR, and NOT. Yes, your Boolean operators should be typed in all capital letters. "OR" is expansive, it will increase your results. The use of "AND" and "NOT" is reductive, they reduce your results. These terms are going to help you focus on the results you need. So how do they work? Let's take the person who is writing the history paper on women's suffrage as an example. In Google or any other general search engine, you would just type in "women's suffrage," cross your fingers, do your lucky dance, and hope for the best. In a library database, you are going to get better results by typing in "women AND suffrage." That is going to bring up all the results that have to do with both women and suffrage. Maybe your patron wants to exclude results from the Australian suffrage movement (American women were not the only ones fighting for the vote). If that's the case you can enter the search string "women AND suffrage NOT Australia." This is going to narrow your results even further. Now let's remove the Brits, "women AND suffrage NOT Australia NOT British." Now your patron has narrowed their results to exactly what they want. "OR" works similarly. If your patron wants information on the women and black suffrage movements they can enter "(Women OR Black) AND suffrage" and get the results they are looking for. Did you notice the parentheses? If you are "OR"ing two or more things, you need to use the parentheses for the computer to recognize those topics should be together if you have an "OR" followed by an "AND" or "NOT."

Now we're going to up your game one notch. We're going to talk about truncation. Let's say you have someone writing a paper on ethics (one of my favorite subjects). There are a lot of words that could be used that are similar when researching; ethic, ethics, ethical, ethicist. Sure, you could type "ethic OR ethics OR ethical OR ethicist," but that seems like a lot of work. Surely there's an easier way. There is, it's called truncation. In truncation, we would take that search string and simplify it by putting in the root word followed by the truncation symbol. (This, unfortunately, varies based on the database, but they could be *, !, ?, or #. The "help" section of the database will tell you which one it is) So, you would type in "ethic*" and that will cover all four of the search terms. However, if you type in "eth*" you are going to be searching for every word that starts with "eth" including ethanol, ethane, ethereal, and so many others that are unrelated to ethics, so choose where your truncation goes wisely. Truncation can also be used in the middle of a word as well. In our women's suffrage example, what if you wanted to search for women and woman? Well, with truncation you could substitute the truncation symbol for the change in the vowel, "wom*n" covers both words. Same thing with the differences in American and British English, color and colour mean the same thing, one is the American spelling, the other is the British, but you can truncate it by typing in "colo*r."

Once you have a handle on operators and truncations, you need to understand stop words. These are the words that don't bring much to the table, as far as your search goes. They typically are a, an, the, in, of, on, are, be, if, into, and which. These words are too common to be effective in a search. If the database search included these words in its results, your results would be flooded with irrelevant information. Just because most databases omit results for these words doesn't mean they always do. So, there are a couple of exceptions you should be aware of. First, if the word is a part of a controlled vocabulary or descriptor. For example, the "of" in the United States of America is part of this controlled vocabulary so that "of" becomes important and is usually included. Second, you have the ability to have many databases ignore the stop word protocol. To do this you can include the stop word in quotations. So if you are looking for results about Tolkien's master work, *The Lord of the Rings*, you can type in: Lord "of" "the" Rings, and the stop words would be recognized.

With operators, truncations, and stop words understood, you're well on your way to being a searching pro and can tackle ninety-five percent of what you will ever encounter. If you want to dive deeper into database searching, you'll need to learn about phrases, fields, and the difference between keywords and subjects. However, those topics are going to take care of the additional five percent of what you may encounter. You can dive into those when you have a little (or a lot) more experience using databases. I'm trying to get you going, so go start by using those operators, truncations, and stop words.

Earlier I talked about how for the majority of your interactions you would probably be better off just using your standard search engine in a browser, your Googles and Bings. When you have someone who is looking to be pointed in the right direction about a topic there are a couple of things you have at your disposal as well. Some library databases have topic overviews included in them. These are little articles that have a ten-thousand-foot view of the subject. What they also usually have is a bibliography at the end that your patron can use to dive deeper into the subject. What if the databases your library subscribes to don't have this feature? I like to default to Wikipedia. That's right, the very same place that every high school teacher and university professor tells their students isn't a viable source. And those people are right. If you're looking for academic sources to use in a paper, Wikipedia isn't a good one. Anyone can go in and make changes to it at any time so the resource is never the same and wrong information could be populated into the result. However, this resource can give your patron an overview of the topic and if you scroll to the bottom of the results for the topic, you'll find a bibliography of the source material. You can use this list just like the database topic overviews and pull some great source material for your patron. Problem solved.

Whenever you're helping a patron search for material, keep in mind that information literacy is just like reading literacy. It is something learned and, unfortunately, most people don't practice very often, so have some patience with your patron. Additionally, part of helping library patrons understand information literacy is ensuring that multiple perspectives are available for people to engage with. In our contemporary culture, people tend to stay in information silos. These silos often effectively stifle opposing information, in essence making the information someone is engaging with one-sided. As a library employee, you can help your patron be well informed by ensuring they have access to opposing information so they can review it all and take an informed position. Therefore, if someone is searching about climate change, make sure you include information that explores the evidence that it is happening as well as the arguments that it isn't. Present them with access to all the relevant information. Whether or not they engage with it is their decision. That may really get your blood boiling, but understand that as a library employee your job isn't to make your personal opinion or bias known to your patron, it is to ensure they have the information to come up with their own conclusions.

As a last request for this chapter, I'd like you to pull up your local library's website or go into their branch and see what databases they have. Play around with them. Chances are they have some great resources you didn't even know you had access to. Literary reference centers; historical databases full of world, national, regional, and even local history; home improvement reference resources; mailing lists for new businesses; access for business owners to see information about their competitors; genealogical research resources; medical databases; car repair manuals; and likely so much more is probably available at your fingertips. When you understand everything your library has to offer, you will be better positioned to help patrons with what they need.

CHAPTER SIX

Community Connection

Connecting to the community happens in one-on-one interactions at a public library every day. However, those aren't the connections that this chapter is going to focus on (if you're looking for information on those see the chapter on Service and Patrons). This chapter is going to be about connecting with other community organizations.

The long-term success of a public library rests on those who work for the library not only connecting to individual patrons but also connecting with other key organizations in the community. Connecting with the local schools, Boys and Girls Clubs, United Way, Rotary organizations, Chamber of Commerce, government organizations, and many other groups that exist in the community will bolster the institution's ability to have the greatest impact on their patrons. Many of these organizations have the overall health and vibrancy of the community as one of their primary concerns—that aligns directly with many public libraries' objectives.

Because many organizations' objectives align so closely with the goals of public libraries, some unique and mutually beneficial partnerships can be formed. Partnering with the Chamber of Commerce can help the library show entrepreneurs how libraries can help businesses. In return, those entrepreneurs have expertise in areas that may make great library programs. Those programs, ultimately, position that local business owner as a subject matter expert in our community, leading to more business for them. It becomes a cycle that benefits the community, and you, as a library employee, can feel good about helping a local business owner find a new audience.

I have personally partnered with the Small Business Development Center, two historical societies, a local finance blogger, an employment agency, a freelance education advisor, a league of local authors, a local publisher, human resource managers from businesses all over town, the Chamber of Commerce, local banks, the English club at the local community college, and so many other groups, always with success. Many of my contacts were formed before I came to work at the library, but not all of them. So, if you don't have a big pile of people you can call on from groups all over town who you've formed relationships with already, how do you start?

Call them up and introduce yourself, say you work for the library and see what happens. Many times people are enamored with the seemingly novel idea of speaking to someone who works for the library and it acts as a great icebreaker. Recently, I had a dental hygienist so taken with the fact I worked at a library that she had to tell me what her favorite books were and why while I was sitting immobile in the chair getting my routine cleaning. The best part of that was seeing her passion for books and not having to admit that I do not, in fact, cannot, list my favorite books without being directed into a narrower criterion. Let them know you are from the library and you are looking to form a relationship with their organization. Most often they get excited about the prospect. I have only had one encounter that seemed less than enthused about my call, and that was just because they didn't know how they would fit in until I laid out some possibilities for them; then they were all-in. I have done cold call sales for retail before, that's not fun. Calling from the library to form partnerships is among the most fun category of phone calls I've ever made. Even if it is a hard "No" it's still a pleasant interaction and you have a great conversation with a local patron in your community.

    Now that you've introduced yourself, I want you to think about the concept of reciprocity. For those of you who have forgotten, or never taken, your psychology class, that is the expectation that people will help those who have helped them. Lucky for you, the library's primary function is to help people. That puts you in a prime position to talk about what the library can do for their organization. I like to start by asking what problems they've encountered that we may be able to help them with. Maybe it's coming up with a mailing list of people who have recently moved to the area for their upcoming fundraising campaign. I have a database that will do that. Maybe it is helping one of their employees become more proficient in Microsoft Excel. I've got a training program for that and can also answer direct questions about specific issues. Maybe it's increasing their organization's profile. I can help them put together a program for the public that will talk about an area of their expertise. Bingo. Now we're scratching each other's backs!

The great thing about forming that first connection with an organization outside the library but in your community is that they will talk with other organizations. The Chamber of Commerce will talk to the Builders and Contractors Association and you have a builder reaching out to you to put together a Home Maintenance 101 class for the library in the fall. Then the person from the Builders and Contractors association has a cousin who is an arborist the next town over who wants to do a pruning workshop. Everything snowballs. Your community members meet experts who are in their backyard, the library gets great content from experts, and you help local businesses thrive. Win, win, win!

The key to keeping the snowball rolling is keeping in touch with those community partners. Visit their events. If the Chamber of Commerce is having a luncheon, go to the luncheon, shake some hands, talk with those business owners, see where you can help them, thank them for their support, and leave them smiling! Follow up on any need they may have. If you tell them you can help them set up their Google Business listing, you better make that happen or they will remember that you dropped the ball. Remember, just because they are a business owner doesn't mean they aren't part of your patron base. In fact, commercial property taxes are often multiples higher than residential property taxes, and most public libraries are funded through those property taxes. Those business owners may not be your heaviest users, but they are your largest contributors and if you address their needs too, they have long memories.

The library can also serve as a conduit to bring other community organizations together. Libraries are all about bringing the community together, aren't they? Maybe you hear the local Rotary is trying to raise money to help fund a women's shelter that is struggling.

Maybe you also heard that the Lyon's club is looking for a really meaningful organization to apply the money they raised in their last fundraiser. Perhaps you can get the two organizations talking together and the Lyon's club will help out the women's shelter that has the immediate need and the Rotary will help them with their next fundraiser in return. Now you're quilting together organizations and people into a community to solve problems. That is what makes a strong community, and those organizations will remember that the library helped to make it happen. That's yet another way libraries bring value into a community.

Local schools are also really important to have a good relationship with. Not only are public libraries intimately involved in helping parents with preschool preparation, but they also assist with summer programs designed to help mitigate "summer slide" throughout that long summer vacation. Libraries need to be aware of where the schools need help and it's equally important for the schools to know how they can support the library. When you're dealing with youth populations it truly takes a village, and schools and libraries fulfill similar needs at different times. Schools can help promote programs for children and teens and libraries can reinforce what students are learning in school. Additionally, good communication between schools and libraries can help to mitigate behavioral issues and give each other a heads-up on trends they are seeing. Every minute you spend cultivating this relationship will be well spent and save you time and effort in the long run.

CHAPTER SEVEN

Privacy

Privacy is a huge deal in all types of libraries, but it becomes more difficult when you are a public library. In academic, medical, law, or school libraries there are limitations to who has access acting as a preliminary guard to protect patron privacy. Then there are also other safeguards that are built into those institutions and laws like the Family Educational Rights and Privacy Act that they can leverage to help guide their actions. Public libraries are for everyone, there is no gatekeeper limiting access, and that means the attention of people who work in them needs to be that much more focused.

Luckily for those who work in public libraries, the American Library Association hasn't left us without some guidance. The Library Bill of Rights was first adopted in 1939 and directs how public libraries address this vital component of service. This is what its current iteration says: "All people, regardless of origin, age, background, or views, possess a right to privacy and confidentiality in their library use. Libraries should advocate for, educate about, and protect people's privacy, safeguarding all use data, including personally identifiable information." That's a powerful statement.

It is that statement that has led to librarians being one of the most trusted professions in our society. Think about it; there are people out there who tell library staff that they have cancer before they tell their family members. They trust us to help them through the Social Security website, apply for unemployment benefits, search for jobs, draft legal documents for their divorce, and also help them find materials and resources for the most personal of subjects. However, it only takes one library employee acting with abandon to erode that level of trust.

So what is privacy in a public library? What is a reasonable expectation for a patron to have in a public place? What exactly is "personally identifiable information"? Do children have the same expectation of privacy? What can we, as library employees, do to ensure that we protect our patrons' privacy and personal information? Let's get into it, shall we?

When we talk about privacy in a library context, the first thing that comes to mind is books (and other forms of media). Yep, the cornerstone of the library's very existence happens to be the first thing we are going to cover. In the conversation surrounding privacy and books, I want you to imagine the following scenario. A young woman comes up to your checkout counter to check out several books about how to remove yourself from an abusive relationship and see if she can place a hold on a couple more about the same topic. You saw how pensively she approached you and you can hear the apprehension in her voice so you are very careful to stay professional, deal with her with compassion while ensuring that you stay composed, provide her a pamphlet on some local organizations she can also reach out to, and place the items she needs on hold. Great interaction, right? That's an example of helping someone the way we as library employees hoped to be able to when we signed on to do our jobs. Let's follow it through. An item the young lady requested arrived and a member of the staff calls the phone number on the account to let her know. A man's voice answers the phone and kindly says the young lady is unavailable and he would be happy to pass on a message. The library employee informs him that one of the items she placed on hold has arrived and is ready to be picked up. The man cordially asks what item it is and the library employee reads off a title, *Escaping the Maze of Abuse*. The next day, the young woman comes into the library, with the hood up on her sweatshirt trying to cover the bruises on her face, and dumps the books she checked out in the book drop before turning right back around and leaving without picking up the items she had requested.

That scenario may sound like hyperbole, but these types of things do happen. Did the staff member making that phone call intend on causing any harm? No. But their lack of awareness toward patron privacy for that single moment caused an issue that was unintended and likely unrepairable. Countless topics could be applied to this scenario. Every day, library staff in rural and urban libraries alike deal with people who are questioning their sexuality, exploring pregnancy options, looking to end relationships, seeking different religious beliefs, and countless other topics that some people may find controversial and could potentially create a volatile situation. Libraries are supposed to be a place where the free exploration of ideas and information can be engaged with. Privacy facilitates that goal.

That expectation of privacy applies to library staff as well. Patrons should be able to engage with material and resources in the library without having to worry about library staff peeking over their shoulders or reviewing their accounts to assess their reading habits. Not only is the freedom to explore, question, and inquire impeded when people feel like they are being monitored, the ability to assess content, consider arguments, and make personal determinations is affected as well. The expectation of privacy found in public libraries protects patrons' ability to read, think, and decide for themselves what they believe and value.

It is this expectation of privacy that has driven the way libraries deal with patron information. I once had a patron who wanted to read the manifesto of Ted Kaczynski, that's right, the Unabomber. Honestly, that request wouldn't be all that unusual at an academic library, many scholars have studied it intensively for many different reasons, but for some reason, this patron felt that this was a strange request, maybe because it was a public library. I asked him what his concerns were in requesting the item and he replied that he didn't, "want to end up on a terrorist watch list." The great thing about that fear is it is easily overcome. Forty-eight states and the District of Columbia have statutes that declare library records are confidential documents; the two states that don't have statutes have opinions from attorneys general' that reinforce library records as confidential documents. The intent behind these declarations and opinions is to assure the public that no person can come under suspicion simply because they read a book or researched a topic. Because you read the manifesto of Timothy McVeigh doesn't mean you are going to go on a bombing spree.

To take this one step further, most libraries purge patrons' checkout history once it is no longer necessary to keep it. For example, when you return an item at the library where I work, it removes it from your patron record. This confuses some patrons. On many occasions, I've had patrons call looking for recommendations thinking I can just pull up their account and view the history of their checkouts to make a recommendation. I can't of course because, for better or worse, I don't have that information. This is one of those instances where convenience and privacy are in opposition. Sure, it would be convenient for me to be able to view your history to make a recommendation, but being able to do that makes it so your record could be obtained if something like the security of library systems was ever compromised or also through a court-ordered subpoena. In fact, the American Library Association has specific guidance on this too. One of their key talking points about patron privacy states, "Librarians maintain records to ensure the efficient operation of the library, not to review or document individuals' reading habits. Libraries do not keep or maintain print or electronic records as a means of law enforcement."

Part of the reason this information is purged is that when you look at someone's checkout history, you can start to piece together who someone is. This is a form of "personally identifiable information." Over a lifetime, our reading habits become like a fingerprint—unique and varied. What we read (or the other media we engage with) inevitably helps us to form our unique intellectual identity. Knowing this history becomes information that paints an intimate portrait of the person engaging with it. I don't know about you, but I would like to choose who I let know me that intimately and it's a part of my job to share with others what I read, at least to some extent. You don't have to be doing something nefarious to not want others having access to something so personal, so as library workers we protect the patrons' right to share that information with only those they want to.

Everything surrounding privacy up to this point has discussed intellectual privacy, but what level of physical privacy should a patron be able to expect in a public library? It's unreasonable for someone to expect that they won't be seen by others who are also in the library. It is a "public" library, after all. However, as library employees, we also have a responsibility not to disclose who is using our facilities. You shouldn't be tabulating who is coming and going and when as a matter of course. So when would this come up? Well, if a patron comes up and asks if John Doe is in the library, if you aren't keeping tabs, you can honestly say you don't know.

Another aspect of physical privacy is ensuring that patrons have access to places where they can sit and engage with library materials without being on display for everyone. Many portions of public libraries are now designed to be conducive to collaboration. Big tables, groupings of chairs, and other arrangements seem to be directly opposed to facilitating someone having enough privacy to feel comfortable reading a book on a controversial topic. And these arrangements are more and more frequent in the modern public library. We, as library employees, need to ensure that there are spaces in the library where someone can feel comfortable by themselves.

Physical privacy extends to how you interact with a patron's information too. As a library employee, you have access to your patrons' names, addresses, phone numbers, email addresses, and often familial relationships. Don't abuse that access by looking up to see how much the house they live in is worth just because they balked at having to pay $6.99 to replace a book they damaged—that is completely unprofessional.

When we look at these aspects of intellectual and physical privacy, at what age do they reasonably start? We can turn to the American Association for School Libraries for some guidance here, since their focus is primarily on children. They state, "The library community recognizes that children and youth have the same rights to privacy as adults." That's pretty clear but not necessarily pragmatic. A lot of this depends on the individual library's policies. At the library where I work, we don't have age requirements to get a library card. A mother of an infant can come in and sign up their child for a library card, in fact we encourage it. However, it becomes increasingly difficult to manage the day-to-day maintenance of a card when you can't speak or even walk. This situation must allow some leeway in letting the responsible party manage the account. On the other hand, perhaps you have a teenager who has checked out some books to assist them in assessing their sexual orientation. They should have a reasonable expectation that you aren't going to "out" them to Mom or Dad, and you should protect their privacy, regardless of your personal opinions.

Knowing all these aspects of privacy, how do you work with them in mind in the day-to-day operations of a library? Simple, if you aren't dealing with the patron, err on the side of caution. Let's look back at the staff member who disclosed the title of the book the young woman experiencing abuse had placed a hold on. All that staff member needed to do when asked the title of the item was simply state, "Unfortunately, I can't divulge that information to anyone other than the cardholder, but if you could please let them know we have an item here waiting for them, we would appreciate it." That's all you have to say. There is no identifying information divulged, it's ambiguous. We can make sure any item that has identifying information like names, phone numbers, and lists of items a patron is waiting for are disposed of properly when we are done with them, usually in a shredder. We can also assess the way our spaces in the library are set up to ensure there is space people can use to privately engage with library material. Finally, and most importantly, make sure you understand and follow your library's policies and procedures when it comes to patron privacy. Those policies and procedures are in place not only to protect your patrons but also you as the library employee.

CHAPTER EIGHT

Collection Management

You may think that as a newly minted public library employee you will have little to do with collection management. If that's your understanding, I'm about to flip your world upside down. In most libraries, the person who has the largest impact on the management of the collection is often the person who is shelving the materials. That person is often among the newly hired employees of the library or a high school or college student working the evenings after their classes are over. Let's take a moment to explore why they have such a large impact on collection management.

The person shelving items has the largest opportunity to fix things throughout the library. They weave their way up and down the stacks, return things to the obscure corners, and generally cover every square inch of the collection every time they work. They are touching every item that was returned as well as engaging with the shelving locations where those items belong. That's a lot to put on one person's shoulders—or in a medium to large library several people, but you get the idea.

What I'm about to say may be a surprise to some, but here it goes. To work in a library you have to know your alphabet and your numbers. That's right, I'll say it again. Know your alphabet. Know your numbers. There are some days when it seems like people forget. This was never more evident than when access to the stacks was limited during the Covid-19 restrictions of 2020. One of the first things the staff where I work did was go through every shelf to get them back in order. With the assumption that our patrons were the ones who grabbed something from over here and then put it in the wrong spot over there, we attacked this task with zeal. We knew that it was going to be a while before patrons would return to roaming the stacks. What happened in the weeks (and, unfortunately, months) to come was the collection saw things slowly migrate back to being out of order. It wasn't the patrons, because they had no access to the stacks. It was us. Library employees (GASP) were getting it wrong, and an ounce of humility broke through our hubris.

This may seem elementary, but I'm going to stand on a soapbox for just a moment to talk about the importance of making certain things are where they should be. If things aren't where they are supposed to be, your patrons can't find them. Staff also wastes a lot of valuable time they could use for something that adds more value to their communities. Searching out items that were last seen two days ago, but aren't where they should be, is a major frustration. If items can't be found, they may need to be reordered, at an additional expense that could be used for something else. It is in everyone's best interest to take the time to make sure things are shelved correctly.

So, what does shelving things correctly look like? Much of that is going to depend on the individual library and, hopefully, you will be paired up with a guide in the first few days of your employment to show you some of your particular library's quirks. Even the individual libraries in our library district have certain things they do differently that are location-specific. Remember, we approach everything we do with the end user in mind, which may be different depending on the community. However, you can learn a lot just by walking up and down the stacks of your library and paying attention.

The first thing you need to know is what classification system your library uses. There are three main ones. The most widely used in the Western world is the Dewey Decimal Classification or DDC. This is the one that most k-12 schools and public libraries in English-speaking cultures are going to use (it's also been translated into over thirty languages). It originated in the United States, so we're pretty proud of it. You likely have been exposed to it since elementary school. The second possibility is the Universal Decimal Classification or UDC. This classification system is pretty popular abroad and is multilingual which is why you will find it more frequently in non-English speaking parts of the world. Finally, we have another one that originated in the United States, the Library of Congress Classification or LCC. Ironically, public libraries in the United States rarely use this one; it's more commonly used in academic libraries across the globe. Once you know which classification system your library uses, you can begin to understand how the collection is managed. To help you along, I'll give a brief overview of how the classification systems work.

Dewey Decimal Classification:

Since this is the one you are most likely to encounter, it's going to be the longest review of the three. Created by Melville Dewey in 1873 and published in 1876, it is designed to have the flexibility to expand into topics we aren't even aware exist yet. It uses a number classification that corresponds with basic subjects. These numbers stem from ten main classes and then break out into sub-classes that they call the "second summary" then that summary breaks out into another one called the, you guessed it, "third summary" and it keeps getting broken down as far as necessary. It can be really helpful, especially when aiding patrons, for library employees to know at least the main classes and, depending on how good your memory is, possibly even the second summaries. I've included a chart that details out these in the appendix.

Within the Dewey Decimal Classification, every book, movie, audio recording, or any other type of media falls into a particular category. That category has a location assigned based on the number assigned to its classification and the author's last name. This all looked much simpler when Melvil Dewey published his idea in 1876. There just wasn't the plethora of items or types of media available that we have now. What many public libraries actually do, the one where I work included, is separate out portions of those classifications to be housed by themselves. An easy example that most people relate to is separating the "Fiction" from the "Nonfiction." In actuality, if you stay true to the classification form, fiction should be located in the 800 class, but in practice, most public libraries separate at least most of the fiction into a section of their own (they may leave behind canonical works, poetry, humor, and short stories in the Dewey area). My library also has a separate section for magazines, journals, and serials which technically should be in the 050 second summary, and biographies which should be in the 920 second summary. Our DVDs, audiobooks, music recordings, and genre fiction are also separated into their own sections.

The reason libraries break sections out like this is simple, it's more patron friendly. Public libraries generally focus on ensuring circulation (people checking items out for use) isn't impeded. They become a blend of a library, which in the traditional sense is a repository of materials, and a bookstore that is trying to promote people to take something home with them. They don't want items sitting year after year on their shelf unused. More on that later.

When working within your library's Dewey section, you will have a number and then the author's last name, usually printed on a label on the spine, to help you find where the item belongs. To make sure things are filed correctly, follow the following order of operations:

1. Dewey Decimal Classification Number, filed in numerical order.
2. Author's surname (last name), in alphabetical order.
3. Author's first name, in alphabetical order.
4. Title in alphabetical order.

There are a few things to keep in mind. First, the numbers in the Dewey Decimal Classification work just like they do in math class ("1.1234" is larger than "1.1"). Since we file things on the shelf left to right, top to bottom, smaller number to larger number, "1.1" will be placed on the shelf first with "1.1234" after it, regardless of the name of the author or the title of the work. It doesn't matter how many zeros exist after the decimal point either. For example "40" is

83

the exact same as "40.000" when it comes to where it goes on the shelf. In older libraries, you may find both types of labels exist in the same collection because, as the collection was added to over the years, they either started including the numbers to the right of the decimal point or omitted them because they were unnecessary. If you encounter this, treat both of them as just another "40" and move on to the next thing you need to consider, the surname, to put it in its correct place.

Author names have a few things you need to be aware of as well. Nothing always comes before something. "De Gaulle" comes before "Degas." Why? Because there is a space in the surname "De Gaulle" three characters in, and that space is "nothing," so it goes first. It works the same way when the nothing appears at the end of the name, like with the names "Michael" and "Michaelson," "Michael" will always come first. Also, "Mc" and "Mac" are different. "Mac" comes before "Mc" because the second character of "A" comes before "C." Also, authors from cultural backgrounds different from the Western culture we typically associate with in the United States, Great Britain, and other countries that were under the influence of ancient Rome may have their surname first and their given name last. I'm looking at you Hungary, Austria, parts of Germany, China, both Koreas, Japan, Vietnam, Cambodia, Lao, South India, Sri Lanka, and Madagascar. Often when a publisher picks up a foreign author's book, they will publish it with this in mind and flip the surname to be in the last position when published in a region that has what we in the West would consider "normal" naming conventions; however, that isn't always the case. Take South Korean author Un-su Kim for example. In his native South Korea, his books have his name published in the traditional Korean format with his surname first, so his books are authored by Kim Un-su. In the United States, his books are published under Un-su Kim. Regardless of your position on the cultural sensitivity of such action, you should be aware that not all publishers move the surnames to the end and the surname for this particular author should be under "Kim", not Un-su, no matter which one comes first.

When it comes to first names, you need to make sure they follow alphabetical order too. There is nothing more frustrating than trying to find a "Susan King" book in the middle of the "Stephen King" section, or worse yet, the "Steven King" in with "Stephen King". In that scenario, all of Stephen King's books should come first, followed by Steven King's, followed by Susan King's. Each author is grouped together.

Finally, we come to the weirdness of titles. When it comes to filing the titles in alphabetical order, there are special things to consider. Items get filed by title with "significant" words. If your book title starts with the word "The," which is not considered a significant word, you move on to the next word. Insignificant words include articles such as "a," "an," and "the." Prepositions, on the other hand, are included in the alphabetization, so "of," "for," and "into" are used as you alphabetize the title. Abbreviations are also filed as depicted, not as the word they abbreviate. For example, "Mr." is filed exactly as it is shown, not as "mister". Numbers also come before letters, so *100 Ways to Die* as a title comes before *One Hundred Mishaps* and even before *Aaron's Dilemma*.

With all of these things understood, you should be able to effectively work within a library that has based its collection placement on the Dewey Decimal Classification. Remember that the library you work in will likely have its own way of doing things that you will figure out as you are on-boarded. They are going to place their collection based on the needs of their patron base, so stay amenable to working with the system that works for your community.

Universal Decimal Classification:

If you really look at the Dewey Decimal Classification system, you'll notice that it is very oriented toward Western civilization with a Christian background. If you look at the Religion class, you will find that ninety percent of it is devoted to the Christian religion. If you look at the Language class, you will see that seventy percent is devoted to European languages. The Literature class devotes eighty percent of its span to either American or European literature. For members of societies who are neither Western nor Christian, the system itself illustrates the innate bias that omits their cultures. The Universal Decimal Classification system is one answer to counter that innate bias. It was specifically designed to be used internationally.

Like the Dewey system, the Universal Decimal Classification system uses a numerical classification system. Its representation of this numerical classification takes a slightly different tack. It has a three-digit string, a decimal point, another three-digit string, a decimal point, and a final three-digit string. So it looks like this: 123.456.789. Also similar to Dewey, it is broken down into ten main tables (schedules), with room for expansion as needed, followed by auxiliaries that include things like Language, Form, and Place. A chart showing the ten main tables is shown in the appendix for your reference as well. When items are shelved, just like with Dewey's system, you go by the number first (you take each of the three blocks of numbers, in turn, left to right), then the author, and finally the title.

Very few public libraries, at least in the United States, use this classification system. However, I do find it on items that I interlibrary loan from other libraries, particularly those that are based out of seminaries (more on interlibrary loans later in this chapter). I'm not going to go into much detail here because for ninety-nine percent of whoever may read this, this classification isn't going to apply and the creators of it consulted with Dewey himself, so much of it mirrors his ideas.

Library of Congress Classification:

Academic libraries in the United States and many abroad use the Library of Congress Classification so I'm not going to spend much time here either since I'm focusing on public libraries in this book. You'll be able to find a chart detailing the letters and titles of the main classes in the appendix along with the others. Unlike the Dewey and Universal systems, the Library of Congress Classification is alphanumeric. The call number on the spines of these books will have four lines. The first two lines are going to correspond with the subject of the book, the third line is going to represent the author's last name, and the last line represents the date of publication.

If you happen to be in a library that uses this classification system and are tasked with shelving these items, keep in mind that you do so by going line by line. The first line goes in alphabetical order, the second line is read as a whole number and gets filed in numerical order, the third line is alphanumeric so go by the letter first and then by the number, and the final line is the date so file from oldest on the left, most recent to the right.

Now that we're through the classification systems and how they are arranged on the shelves, let's explore some of the other ways you may be involved in collection management.

Weeding the Stacks:

As I stated before, public libraries aren't just a repository of items. The items they hold need to circulate. If public libraries were a private retail business we would be talking about sales per square foot and how to assess what is driving your average ticket, but public libraries walk a delicate line between a repository and a business that needs to move product. That means periodically the collection is assessed to ensure that it reflects the needs of the community. There are a couple of principles that are considered when making these decisions.

How often the item circulates is one of the largest considerations. An item that is always getting checked out is likely to stay in the collection. Where I work, we don't consider removing items that have been checked out in the last two years unless there is another concern, like the condition of the item. Many of these items are the most popular in the collection and will stay that way for years on end.

Another consideration, particularly in nonfiction, even if the item doesn't circulate very well, is if the item offers an alternative position to one that is more widely held. That may be a tough pill for you personally to swallow, but you have to remember that librarians don't take sides on issues. Patrons need to be able to find books on evolution as well as intelligent design, no matter what your personal beliefs or what the widely accepted position is. With this in mind, topics that are of current concern would be climate change, class divisions, alternative medicine, dieting, socialism vs.

capitalism, gender identity issues, and even political polarization. One hundred years from now, those topics will likely have changed, but the fact that libraries are a place where you can engage in all aspects of an argument on a topic shouldn't.

The condition of an item can often be a deciding factor as well. If bindings are broken, pages are falling out, or in the case of DVDs and CDs they are so scratched they are unplayable, those items need to be assessed for repair or removal from the collection. Not only do items in disrepair not get checked out very often, when they do the patron has a poor experience with them, which they associate with your institution. So if you run across something that isn't in good condition, talk with your supervisor about it and see what conditions your library finds acceptable and what you do with items that don't meet the grade.

The type of material can also have a big impact on when it gets weeded. For example, where I work we keep newspapers for three months and magazines for one year. Once something hits its expiration date, we remove it from the system and either put it out for patrons to take home as a freebee, work with the local schools that may want the item, or recycle it. There is likely a similar process that will take place in your public library.

Shelf Maintenance:

I alluded to this earlier in the chapter. Before working in a library I was an operations and administration manager for a big box specialty retailer. On my career path, I took a trip through sales and even served as a sales manager managing and training other sales professionals. Part of my duties was to ensure merchandising standards were upheld in my location. A library isn't much different in that respect. You want your customer, or patron, to be able to find things where they should be, and you want to entice them into grabbing something that they didn't even know they were looking for. In retail, this is called increasing your average ticket. In library land, it is called increasing circulation.

As you walk the stacks in your library, you are going to see things out of place. Put them back where they belong. The average patron doesn't want to mess up your shelves, but many times they just don't know what to do, so they will leave the book lying at the end of a row, set it on a table, or if you're lucky they will put it in a return area. They aren't trying to make your job tougher; they just don't know what to do. Along those same lines, you're going to find trash, scraps of notepaper, items patrons left behind, chairs left in the middle of the aisle, etcetera. Take care of those items too. Remember, part of visiting the library is the experience, not just the goal of borrowing a certain item, so work to make that experience as pleasant as possible.

Your library probably has some standards that they put in place and want to see executed regularly. Maybe they want all the books lined up with the front edge of the shelf (in retail we called this "facing" an aisle). Perhaps they want to display books facing cover out on the right-hand side of each shelf that is at eye level. They may want those books that have the covers facing out placed in a holder (it is hard on the spines to just crack them open a little and let the front and back covers do the work). There's probably an area where the staff makes regular displays that will need restocking. Whatever those merchandising standards are for your library, find out what they are and keep them in mind as you go through the stacks. If the library doesn't have formalized merchandising standards, you can help to make them formal. Ten items that need reviewed for merchandising standards each day is a manageable number and can make a big difference to the patrons' experience in a very short amount of time. All of these things are a part of collection management too.

The last thing I'll cover in this section is shelf reading. Some people find they love shelf reading, others find they loathe it. Either way, it is a task that is crucial to managing the library's collection. You find things that have been missing, things shelved incorrectly, damaged items that need to be reviewed, and most important of all, you are making sure things are easier to find in the long run. So what is shelf reading? It is when you go down the shelf, reading the spine labels of the books, movies, audiobooks, or whatever media you are working with to make sure that the items are in the correct order. You will likely be surprised at how much you find out of place. Willems gets mixed in with Williams, 635.1 gets filed with 365.1, Alex Cross novels are filed under Cross instead of their author, Patterson; stuff happens. We double and triple-check to catch those all-too-common human errors.

Collection Development:

You can devote a whole book to collection development. To be clear, I don't deal with much regarding collection development on the acquisition side; our Technical Services department does most of that. As a new public library employee, you won't likely be charged with this task—at least not at first. However, particularly if you're in a small library, you may have some responsibilities surrounding it. While I don't deal with acquisitions daily, I do request that we purchase certain items for the library based on gaps I see in the collection or new releases I run across that I think our community would appreciate. There is likely some way patrons can request items be purchased for your library's collection as well.

If you find yourself having to make acquisition decisions, keep in mind that you not only want to be bringing in items that are going to be circulating within your patron base, but that you also need to ensure minority and marginalized sections of your community have their interests represented and needs met as well. Sometimes that means bringing in books written in other languages, sometimes it means finding titles that are converted into braille books, other times it means finding LGBTQ+ authors. Whatever it is for your community, you need to make sure those needs are met. You will also likely have to balance between forms of items. Many books are also available as audiobooks and eBooks so deciding on which resources to make available is an important one that should be based on the usage of your community.

One of the misunderstandings outside of the library world is that if a library has an eBook or eAudiobook title in their collection, it can be used simultaneously by multiple individuals for forever. These formats often have licenses for use that get purchased to allow the library to use them. One license permits one use at a time. Some of those licenses extend for the life of the service the library is using to facilitate their management, and others expire after a given timeframe or number of uses. These licenses are often expensive. Many people think that it is similar to when they buy an eBook on Amazon—it's cheaper than the print book—but it can be up to three or four times the cost of the physical item for libraries to add these eBook resources to their collections.

You may be asking yourself where libraries even get their items from. Typically, for books, they get them through a distributor. The most common one we use where I work is Ingram, but we also purchase things through Amazon, Baker and Taylor, and other places as well. For electronic books and audiobooks, we purchase those licenses through the same service we use to manage that collection, OverDrive. We purchase magazines and national newspapers through EBSCO and for local newspapers we go right to the paper for a subscription. Chances are your library has vendors they are already using, so if you find yourself as the person who needs to order materials, there are likely existing avenues for you to leverage.

Once you've procured items, those items will need to be entered into whatever cataloging system your library uses. Most libraries have moved to digital catalogs, but the concept of the digital catalog is the same concept that the card catalogs that used to be used had. Each record is going to contain information about the item such as title, author, subject, shelving location, physical location (if you have multiple branches), type of material, all that type of stuff, and probably even the replacement cost in case a patron loses the item. This type of information becomes what is commonly referred to as metadata. All this metadata is entered into what is called a MARC record. MARC stands for MAchine Readable Cataloging. The machine most often used now is a computer. MARC records are standardized formats in which all the information about an item is stored. They allow libraries to migrate systems and communicate what they have to other libraries for things like interlibrary loans. In your onboarding process, you will likely learn a few basics of cataloging and when the time comes for you to dive into the deep end there are lots of resources that can help you out. A word of caution; the integrity of the catalog for your library is a really important thing. It allows not only the people who work in your building but also those from across the world to know what you have in your collection. If you are cataloging items, make sure you pay close attention and stay consistent with the conventions your library has in place, or you can confuse a lot of people very quickly.

Interlibrary Loan:
Sometimes requests will come in for items that you just can't order. Maybe the item is out of print. Maybe it's still in print but is so obscure that the expense of adding it to the collection doesn't make sense. Maybe it is just flat-out too expensive and doesn't work with your budget. Luckily many libraries have the ability to interlibrary loan items for their patrons. An interlibrary loan is when one library borrows an item from another library to be able to lend it to a patron. Libraries that offer this service to their patrons will have specific systems (usually WorldCat by OCLC) that they use to request items that are shipped to them from other libraries through the mail, UPS, FedEx, or library couriers. There will likely be some training that you will get through the onboarding process that will let you know how your library deals (or doesn't deal) with interlibrary loans. Most libraries that participate are very passionate about getting resources in the hands of those who need them, regardless of where that person is, but they usually don't loan new items. I've spent a lot of time dealing with interlibrary loans for my library and the service is a great way to look like a rock star for your patrons.

As a final reminder, your collection is for your patrons. As a library employee, you are tasked with custodianship of the collection for your community. That isn't a responsibility that should be taken lightly. Your friends, neighbors, family members, and complete strangers have placed their trust in you to make sure that the collection of culture that is housed in your institution, for the benefit of your whole community, is well cared for and made available for use. If you are up to the challenge, you will be rewarded with your community's gratitude.

CHAPTER NINE

Item Repair

Repairing items the library holds in its collection is an eventual inevitability. After all, public libraries hold collections to be used, not to sit on shelves getting dusty (not that other types of libraries let things get dusty, but you get the sentiment). So, when items get damaged, it is often up to the library staff to make the determination of whether an item should be discarded, replaced, or repaired. Remember, this book gives you a ten-thousand-foot view, so there is a lot more for you to learn through experience. Your library will help you learn what you need to know based on what they do. This is just a starting point.

There are all sorts of ways public libraries handle this situation. Much of that is determined by what type of service the library is engaged with in regards to new materials. There are services out there that allow a library to essentially rent an item for a while, at a reduced cost, where the item at the end of that period is returned, in good condition, back to the service. If the item becomes damaged, it is up to the library to pay for the damages rather than send the book back to the service. That cost is often passed on to the patron who borrowed it and caused the damage. However, the model I have more experience with is the model where the library just buys the book for the collection outright. In that case, a library employee has to make a judgment call.

If an item is old, rarely checked out or used, and is damaged beyond what would be feasible to repair, it usually gets discarded. Often we have this item available through one of our other seven locations so we could get it for someone in a day or two if they wanted to engage with it. If it is something that one of our other libraries doesn't hold, we might pop into WorldCat to see if other libraries may hold it, opening us up to the possibility of interlibrary loaning it for a patron if needed. If it truly is something that is extremely local, or even one-of-a-kind, we may consider repairing it to see if we could get a couple more uses out of it.

Before thinking about repairing an item, it's best to think about how you can prevent the damage to begin with. For books, that means covering them. For disk items like DVDs, CDs, and some video games, making sure that the cases are in good condition and that the disk locks in place goes a long way to preventing damage. Whatever you do to prevent damage from the start is easier than trying to fix the damage later.

At my library, mass-market paperbacks get their spines taped, regular fiction paperbacks get a hard plastic cover, nonfiction paperbacks get a soft plastic cover, and the dustcovers for hardcover books are covered in plastic. Every library is different, but we use

Kapco products to protect our books. Pictures or videos are a much more effective way to show you how to protect library books, so I have some videos you can view by following the QR code.

When it comes to repairing library books for a public library, getting a few more uses out of them is the ultimate goal, at least for my library anyway. If a book is going downhill, the binding is coming loose, the cover is worn, there is writing inside, pages are ripped, all the horrors booklovers everywhere may experience, without a complete rebuild—which takes a lot of time and expertise that often makes it more expensive than just buying a replacement—the book is going to continue to deteriorate. We repair books with it in mind that we are hoping to get another half dozen circulations from it before it has to be replaced or discarded. So what types of actions will we take?

We will typically do page reattachments, re-glue a binding, do some extra protection on covers, and erase pencil marks. There are occasions where people have cut out a panel from a graphic novel for example, where we may bring in another copy of the item, photocopy the panel that has been clipped and put it back into place, but that's pretty rare.

To understand how to repair a book, you have to understand how books are bound together. There is a lot to know about bookbinding and you can likely find some great resources in your library's nonfiction section under 686 (Dewey), but I'll cover some of the basics here.

When you talk about binding, there is a big differentiation between paperback and hardcover. Most paperback books that are printed for libraries are what they call perfect bound. We are in an age where authors and publishers can take advantage of print-on-demand services and almost all of these are perfect bound. In addition to being able to be produced in smaller print runs, perfect bound books are lightweight and stack well, making them easy for distributors to ship. They really do solve some legitimate issues that were barriers to the success of self-published authors and smaller publishers alike, so more and more books are coming into libraries with a perfect binding. What exactly does a perfect binding look like?

Perfect binding has each individual page glued into the spine, then the cover is glued around the spine, and the whole thing is trimmed up to create a sharp, crisp, beautifully consistent book. Take a look at the diagram on the next page to more fully understand the mechanics of what is going on.

For all the problems they solve for authors, publishers, and distributors, perfect bound books will not last as long as traditionally bound hardcover books in your library. For the average person buying a book and reading it once, twice, or maybe three times before passing it on to their neighbor to read, a perfect bound book is going to be just fine. However, when you are a library having an item checked out fifty times in its lifespan is not uncommon, and having it dropped in a book return, shipped between locations, sitting on a hot dashboard on a summer day, or having it bounce around in a backpack on its way to and from school is very hard on any type of binding, especially perfect bound books. That being said, perfect bound books are more durable than traditional mass-market paperback bindings which use less glue and lower quality paper.

Perfect Bound Book:

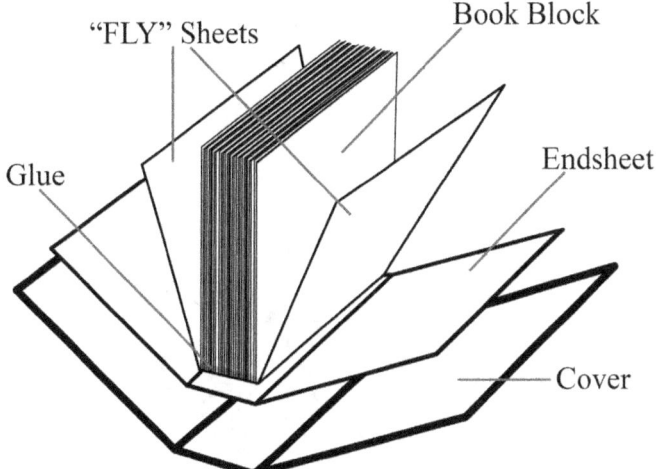

The difficulty in repairing a perfect bound book comes from the fact that each page is individually glued into the book. If one page falls out, it is almost impossible to get it back into place and have it look right. In my library, we use a product called Easy Bind binding tape to take care of these one-off page issues or any issues where we start to see the pages coming apart from the binding. It's not going to look perfect, but it gets the job done so you can check the item out a few more times. You want to make sure you use the Easy Bind on each side of the page to help keep the page in place. If you can tackle the issue while the page is loose, but not entirely free, your results will last longer and look better as well.

Sometimes the binding itself starts to break apart. For a perfect bound book, this is a death sentence. You will not be able to effectively pull them back together to be able to have them circulate many more times.

Hardcover books are more durable but not invincible. They too will have their own issues; however, because they are constructed differently, they are also repaired differently. The pages of hardcover books are usually stitched together in what they call signatures, those signatures are then stitched together and then glued, the spine is covered with a fabric backing material, and then the book is covered with the hardcover. See the illustration below.

Hardcover Bound Book:

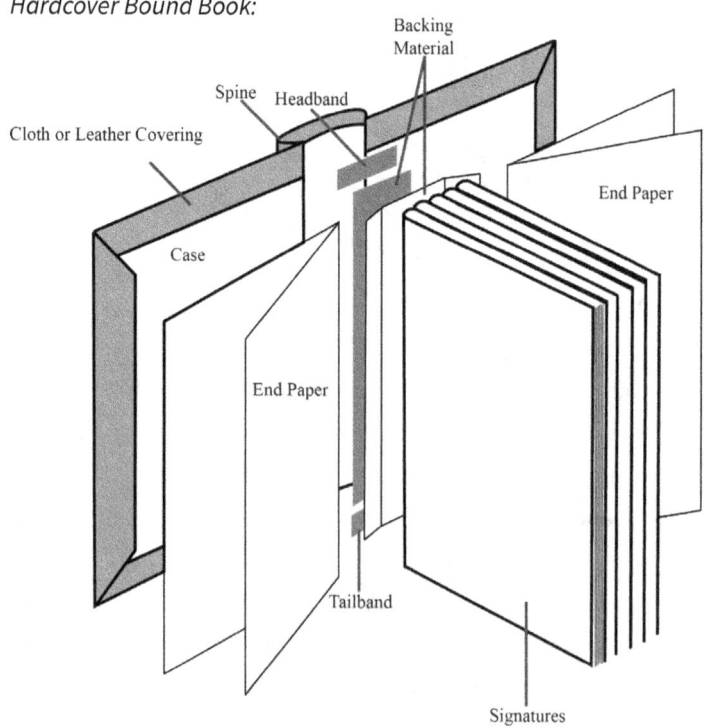

Where the damage is will determine how you fix it. The cool thing is that while pages can be fixed pretty similarly to those of a perfect bound book, although they are far less likely to pop out to begin with, the binding can also be glued back together pretty effectively. The glue you would use is PVA glue made specifically for bookbinding. That glue is acid-free and stays fairly flexible making it great for repairs. If you happen to be gluing a binding back together, make sure you get the glue spread as far down the inside of the binding as you can. Using something like a barbecue skewer can help to get that glue all the way down. Then make sure you put the book into a book press to make sure it dries correctly.

Book Press:

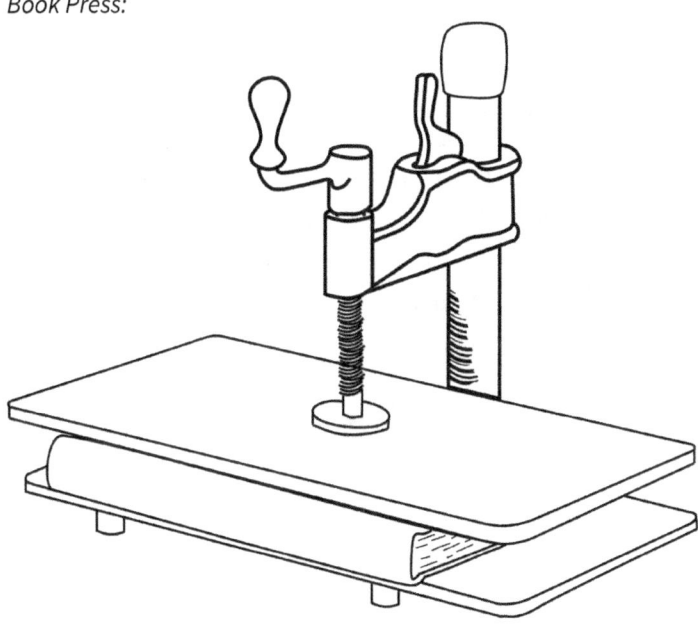

Remember, your goal is to make it so the item can be borrowed a half dozen more times.

When it comes to other materials like CDs and DVDs cleaning them properly can make a big difference. Most libraries have a machine they use specifically to clean these materials. If you don't have access to one of those machines, you can use a soft cotton ball and a little bit of rubbing alcohol and clean the disk from the inside working toward the outer edge in strokes that look like the spokes on a bicycle wheel.

Items like Playaways (self-contained MP3 players with a book downloaded onto them) often just require a battery change. They can also be reset by holding down "SP" and "REV" at the same time. A message will ask if you are ready to reset the Playaway and hit the "Play" button to confirm. The screen will then say "RESET" so you know it has been completed. This usually works, but worst-case scenario Playaway will replace the item for a $15 fee.

There are many other types of items that libraries lend as well. Your library probably has procedures put in place that work for them based on the items they have in their collection. Learning those is going to be important, so think of what you've learned here as a starting point.

CHAPTER TEN

Other Stuff

Facilities

Libraries are increasingly moving into places that are less and less tethered to a specific building. Popup libraries, libraries that are like vending machines, libraries existing in digital space, and so many other creative ideas have pushed the boundaries of where libraries actually operate (we have a "Book Bike" to take around parks for kids in our network). However, unless something really rocks the boat, libraries are still going to be dependent on their facilities functioning as a home base for everything they do. Since we have to rely on those facilities for the foreseeable future, it's a good idea to have a fundamental understanding of what goes into making a facility run.

You don't need to be an expert. Hopefully, your library will have maintenance professionals either on staff or easily available for you to leverage to make sure your facilities stay in great shape to help improve your patrons' experience, but if it doesn't, knowing a little can go a long way. Knowing how to quickly deal with basic issues can give you a sense of confidence that the situation is handled well enough for the professionals to address it without hindering your patrons' immediate experience.

Bathrooms:

Yep, bathrooms can be the biggest pain in your proverbial behind that you may experience in the library. As anyone who has worked in a library very long can tell you some really scary stuff happens in there. Before I go any further, I feel it is important to note that you need to talk with your administrative team and get a clear understanding of how far they want you to go with bathroom issues. Many of the problems that can and do happen have varying degrees of biohazard associated with them. Your administration may require you to go through special training to deal with bodily fluids and may even offer things like hepatitis vaccines for those who have to deal with whatever they may encounter.

Every so often, someone is going to have an accident that is on a level where you will question how they survived. Your patrons don't want to walk in on that. The best thing you can do, regardless of if it is on your list of responsibilities to take care of, is to put your restroom out of order until it is dealt with. Yes, it is a minor inconvenience for your patrons, but if it is bad enough you're considering putting the restroom out of order, they don't want to walk in on it anyway.

If you are tasked with taking care of cleaning up any accidents dealing with bodily fluids, make sure that you are protecting yourself. As much as we care for our patrons and strive to form meaningful connections with them, bodily fluids can carry some very heinous communicable diseases. Hopefully, your library has some basic protections on hand for you to use in these instances. What they are required to have on hand may vary by state, but a pair of gloves, protective booties, face protection, and a Tyvek jumpsuit thrown into a quick response Ziploc would cost around ten bucks and protect you not only from basic hazardous exposures but also protect your clothing from the caustic chemicals you may need to use to clean up the mess to make the area safe and serviceable again. I've ruined at least a couple of pairs of good slacks because I got some bleach on them cleaning up messes in bathrooms at the library—that can get expensive.

As you're cleaning up any messes in the restroom, be sure to look into the areas that aren't always at the forefront of your mind. The junction of the toilet to the floor, the feet of stall dividers, the back of stall doors, the area around toilet paper holders, the cracks of the joints of the flush handles and toilet seat, the next stall over—did I mention sometimes the accidents people have are particularly nasty—all of these areas are easily overlooked if you are just doing a quick pass over the area, but remember that safety and the patrons' experience should be a primary concern. If you're all suited up to deal with the hazards of the situation, you may as well just take care of it all at once and get it over with.

Not all bathroom issues are nasty. Sometimes it's something as simple as a faucet, toilet, or urinal that won't stop running. There's not a big mess to clean up, no clog backing up the drain, just water that won't stop running. There is a water shutoff valve for each plumbing fixture that is in your restroom. It doesn't matter if your library has high-end commercial toilets or the ones they pick up at the hardware store down the street, there is a shutoff valve for the fixture you can turn off. Once off, you can put an "Out of Order" sign on the fixture and let the professionals deal with it. A quick Google search can help you find the supply or shutoff valve for whatever fixture you are dealing with if you don't know where it is already.

If there is a clog backing up a drain and the fixture won't stop running, shut off the supply valve before you try to deal with the backup. If the backup can't be cleared with a plunger, don't try to fix it on your own, reach out to a professional to take care of the situation. With that said, there are different types of plungers you should be using on different types of drains.

Plungers:

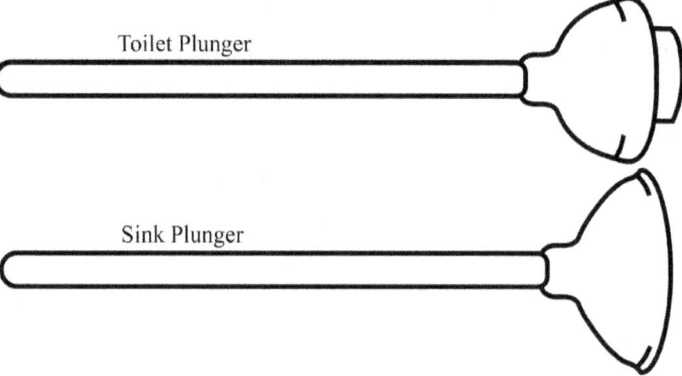

Also, learn where the main water shutoff valve is located and how to shut it off. If you have a sprinkler system, learn where the shutoff valve for that is too (and hope you never have to use it).

If you have issues outside of these, you really should reach out to professionals to get them looked at.

Electrical:

Just like knowing where the shutoff valves for your plumbing system is important, knowing where your electrical breaker panels are is also important. If there is a major issue you need to be able to shut off power to different areas of your building. Also, sometimes the breakers trip when you're trying to do something specific and you need to know where to turn them back on. For example, in one of our meeting rooms if you plug in a coffee maker, a hot water kettle, and then turn on the microwave, it will pop the breaker every time. No matter how many times we tell groups not to do that, there are still a couple every year who do and we have to go turn the breaker back on.

If you have a breaker that is constantly activating, tell your maintenance department. That circuit may be overloaded, or the breaker itself may be wearing out. Either way, the issue should be addressed so it doesn't cause a larger issue.

Other things to consider:

- Don't use extension cords long-term.
- When using extension cords, or any cords for that matter (looking at you mic cords), make sure they are safely out of the way or protected from becoming a tripping hazard.
- You can easily overload a circuit through the use of things like power strips, so use these temporarily and sparingly.

- Never work on electrical fixtures with the power on. If you don't know what you are doing, don't work on them at all. If there is an issue, shut off the breaker to the item and call a professional.

- Cable management is important. Think of all the computers in your library. Effectively managing the cables associated with those resources makes maintenance much easier and you can address issues quicker and more effectively when they arise.

Doors:

Accessibility to the library is a huge concern. If your doors aren't in working order, people with disabilities or mobility issues will find it difficult to use your services. As someone who had a long career in the hardware industry, a grandfather who was a locksmith, and is someone who has installed more doors than they can count, I'm going to say this once; WD40 and other liquid lubricants don't belong anywhere near any door hardware. Door hardware, including hinges and locks, should only have a dry lubricant like graphite. Wet lubricants attract dirt and dust and will eventually make your locks inoperable and your hinges sticky.

Doors will fall out of adjustment over time and through use. If you start to see the gaps between the door and the frame becoming inconsistent, bring it to your maintenance department's attention so they can address it appropriately before it becomes a problem.

Outside:

If you live in an area that has regular weather concerns, make sure you have plans in place to address possible issues. I live and work in an area with long winters and snow is a concern. If you think about the demographics that frequent library locations, a prominent user group is those of retirement age. By the nature of aging in general, mobility issues tend to be more frequent in this group. When you compound those issues with having to walk through snow and over ice, you are asking for an accident to happen. It's not just older patrons that are at risk either, anyone can slip and fall on ice—it's common. Those slips and falls can be damaging and we want all of our patrons to be safe. So, even if you have a contract with someone to deal with weather concerns, like snow removal, you may have to pop outside to clear the main walkways between their visits. Shoveling a path and putting down some ice melt is a lot easier than caring for someone who has slipped, fallen, and injured themselves.

Another thing to consider is how big of an impact taking a walk around your building and picking up trash and debris that was either left behind or blown around by the wind can make. First, it will make your building more inviting to your patrons. Second, it will help to encourage people to help take care of their library. Third, it will discourage those who are prone to leaving behind messes from doing so. It can also alert you to issues you may not have been aware of. I've found bedding underneath bushes, drug-related items, and even people hiding while doing these walks. Your location will have its own mixture of issues you'll find. However, if you don't know what is going on around your building, you don't have a secure location for your patrons to use and you can't help those people who may need access to specific services in your community find those resources.

Finally, and I can't stress this enough, if you feel like you are in over your head, don't proceed blindly. If there is some reason why you can't have a professional take care of the issue, you literally work in a library. Grab a book, check out some YouTube videos, make some phone calls and get it taken care of. Most importantly, if something isn't safe, work to make sure it is. That includes you feeling safe in handling the issue. If you don't feel safe, reach out to someone more comfortable handling it.

First Aid

Knowing some basic first aid is really important. Public libraries deal with a lot of people and many of them are parts of vulnerable populations like the elderly or people experiencing homelessness. The fact is people have medical emergencies and when you work with the public sometimes those emergencies happen in your library. Some of the emergencies that you may encounter include scrapes from kids who took a tumble on their bicycle getting to the library, kids choking, random nose bleeds, trip and fall incidents, diabetic emergencies, seizures, strokes, heart attacks, and even drug overdoses. My recommendation is that you get in touch with a training service like the Red Cross to get some training in first aid and CPR. Knowing what to do and how to handle a situation before you encounter one will give you confidence and sometimes that makes all the difference. Make sure you learn how to apply the basics to adults and children. Your library may have a yearly class they require employees to participate in to keep your knowledge and skills fresh, but if they don't, the American Red Cross has a bunch of videos that you can view online. Take a few minutes to review some of them by following the QR code:

Self-Care

It may sound a little cliché but learning some self-care techniques can also be helpful. Being a public library employee can be stressful. You will hear stories from your patrons that will leave you feeling mentally and emotionally exhausted. You will lose members of your community in tragic ways that will drain every ounce of energy from you. You will deal with frustrating people. Therefore, you need to have the tools to deal with those situations and not let them overcloud all of the wonderful interactions you will also have. Learning what works for you before you need to rely on it is important. For some people meditation or exercise works; for many speaking with a therapist or clergy member does; you may want to express yourself musically, artistically, or through poetry. Find what works as a healthy release for you and make sure you spend the time you need to cultivate it as a habit. Having a healthy habit to turn to when things get tough has benefited many library workers after some really tough days at the library.

CHAPTER ELEVEN

Outlook

The Department of Labor's Occupational Outlook for Librarians states that the profession will grow by about nine percent between 2016 and 2026. Those librarians can expect to make, on average, about $57,680 per year. Keep in mind that we are talking about capital "L" Librarians—so, those with a Master of Library and Information Science degree. That yearly salary is comparable to the national average of a high school teacher who holds a Bachelor's degree and gets three months of the summer away from the classroom—public librarians never get three months every year away from the library, not that they would want it. Library technicians and assistants are slated to see about the same growth, make on average $28,440 per year, and generally just need a high school education to get their foot in the door.

That picture isn't that bad, nine percent growth, average pay that is at least close to the national median income for an American individual. That's the way the Department of Labor paints the picture anyhow. In reality, the picture for public library workers is often quite different.

In the spring of 2016 *Public Libraries Online*, a publication of the Public Library Association, posted an article titled, "Remember When This Was Full-Time? Your Newest Coworkers Don't" by Chris Burns. In this article, Burns discusses the realities of trying to find full-time employment for those who hold a Master of Library and Information Science degree. Often those individuals can only find part-time employment, with little to no benefits, and if they are lucky they can string together a part-time position at a public library and another part-time position at the local community college library to give them the equivalent of full-time hours. They can end up working like that for years on end. Adding to this problem is the fact that library workers with full-time employment usually love their jobs, so they stay put, making turnover nearly non-existent until someone retires.

To be very blunt, I love working at the library, but after working between nineteen and twenty-nine hours per week for two years, I was to the point where I could no longer afford to work for the library and was about to leave when someone retired and I found full-time employment there. Most people can't wait that long. Many people wait much longer. Furthermore, if you can wait that long, you will find yourself up against some stiff competition. I found myself vying for my full-time position against one candidate who held a Master of Library and Information Science and one who is in a Master of Library Science program, both of whom were (and still are) excellent candidates and awesome employees.

Other sectors of library land have taken big hits over the last few years. For example, the public schools in Spokane, Washington laid off their entire workforce of school librarians in the fall of 2019. That means that their sixty-four schools filled with over thirty thousand students are all left without librarians. To be a school librarian requires a Master of Library and Information Science and teaching credentials. Where do you think all those librarians went? They applied for every library position within a fifty-mile radius, including any that were at public libraries, including all part-time positions.

Spokane wasn't alone. Chicago schools reduced their librarian staff from four hundred and fifty to just over one hundred and fifty in 2018. It took them four years to do it, but they did it. The National Center for Education Statistics reported that from 2009 to 2016, over nine thousand full-time equivalent school library positions were eliminated across the United States. That's a fifteen percent reduction. Where did those people go?

At the branch where I work there are twenty-five employees who work there (we also happen to be the district office so I'm not counting the district administrative staff). Of that twenty-five, three are full-time employees. That is only a twelve percent full-time employee percentage, and as far as I'm aware none of us are looking to leave or retire soon. To put that into perspective, when I managed big-box retail stores, our goal was to have a seventy percent full-time workforce with thirty percent part-time to fill in the gaps caused by vacations and other instances that could cause coverage to be thin. Even restaurant workers are employed at a sixty percent full-time to forty percent part-time ratio. My library isn't an anomaly; there are many out there that operate in a similar fashion (but not all). Libraries, in general, have a long way to go.

To be clear, these trends are community-driven and will change based on the community you reside in. Each community, just like everything else, will be reflected in the institution of the library it hosts. I often wonder why my community puts such little value on the expertise library workers provide in helping them look for jobs, learn how to use a computer, find information on their medical diagnosis, fill out legal paperwork, find entertainment, learn new skills, and put on enriching programming for all ages. To be honest, most of the community thinks it's a great government job with tons of benefits, which is true for the twelve percent of us who have full-time employment, but for the other eighty-eight percent it is a difficult slog that they continue with because they love what they do. They often hope to one day get those benefits and afford a middle-class lifestyle. If you work for the public long enough, you will find out that ignorance about local government is often staggering.

There is also a general lack of diversity among library workers as well. The ALA cites that according to the 2009—2010 American Community Survey eighty-eight percent of library workers were white while only roughly sixty-three percent of the population is white. Librarians with disabilities are also few and far between, accounting for only about four percent of the workforce, while just over nineteen percent of the population identifies as having a disability. There are real opportunities for diverse voices to be represented in our institutions.

Conversely, if you are a man, like me, you will also be underrepresented and have to deal with loads of cultural stereotypes. Interestingly enough, men made up ninety-eight percent of the profession through much of the 19th century, now they account for only twenty and a half percent. In an ALA article written by Heidi

Blackburn, Ph.D., titled "Gender Stereotypes Male Librarians Face Today," many of these assumptions are laid right out in the open for librarians to see. Men who work in libraries are often stereotyped as effeminate, socially awkward, antisocial know-it-alls who are quiet, introverted, prudish, uptight, poor-communicating sushers who favor comic books and computer programming. Men do not fit the social narrative of who a librarian is or the romanticized ideal of one—the bespectacled white woman sitting at a reference desk—which has been the stereotype for the last century.

Stereotypes of male library workers can often go in another direction as well, one where the patron assumes that the male library worker is the head administrator (a stereotype I've experienced even though my branch's head librarian is a very capable woman and might be standing right next to me) or that the male library worker is highly proficient at technology use (a stereotype that I have also experienced and can often be reinforced by female library workers).

There is also a portion of the population who associate male library workers as being homosexuals, regardless of how they identify with their sexual orientation. Many people also hold the assumption that male library workers are less effective working with children than female library workers, a stereotype they share with male elementary school teachers. I once applied to work in a children's department and the position was given to another highly qualified candidate. I was given the explanation that I didn't have experience with pre-school-aged children, even though I have been a Cub Scout leader, have two kids, and led build and grow workshops for preschoolers three out of every four weekends at a previous job for five years. It would have been more tactful for them to respond, "We've hired a qualified applicant who has more experience," than to ignore the experience I did have. Men also find themselves moving the heavy stuff around within the library, not that we mind. Despite these stereotypes, the gender pay gap still favors men who are library workers. Women are still paid, on average, seventy-seven cents for every dollar a man is paid.

Don't let me persuade you that men have it particularly bad in libraries—we don't. Women have their fair share of struggles in addition to the pay gap. We often get crank calls that are particularly offensive to women library workers who answer the phone. Often when they put the person on hold and ask a man to speak with the caller, they usually hang up when they hear a male voice. Women also experience their fair share of unwelcomed advances and comments and a disproportionate number of people who generally feel like they can verbally disparage them compared to men. Patrons often assume that it is easier to push around a library employee who is a female to get what they want, especially if what they want is inappropriate.

Do I think it's worth exploring a career working in a public library? The short answer is yes. However, you have to decide for yourself as to in what capacity.

At the beginning of the book I promised I would shed some light on why I haven't gone after obtaining a Master of Library Science degree. Well, the library, for me, isn't my first career. Frankly, the time between where I am now and retirement is short enough that I wouldn't be able to easily justify the investment of time, attention, and money to complete a program and then pay it off. Additionally, my interests are broader than that narrow focus and if I were to dedicate my resources to completing a master's program it would likely be in a similar but adjacent discipline. The answer for you may be different, but you'll never know if you never get started.

This book has been a brief look into the possibilities of what the world of the public library may hold for you if you decide to work in one. Each library is going to have its own way of doing things, but the experiences you have while working for one will have some similarities. So, if after reading all of what is here you think you want to try your hand at working for a public library, go down to your local library and see if they are hiring.

Appendix

Dewey Decimal Classification
- 000 Computer Science, Information, and General Works
- 100 Philosophy and Psychology
- 200 Religion
- 300 Social Sciences
- 400 Language
- 500 Science
- 600 Technology
- 700 Arts and Recreation
- 800 Literature
- 900 History and Geography

- **000 Computer Science, Information, and General Works**
  000 Computer Science, Knowledge, and Systems
  010 Bibliographies
  020 Library and Information Sciences
  030 Encyclopedias & Books of Facts
  040 Unassigned
  050 Magazines, Journals, and Serials
  060 Associations, Organizations, and Museums
  070 News Media, Journalism, and Publishing
  080 Quotations
  090 Manuscripts and Rare Books
- **100 Philosophy and Psychology**
  100 Philosophy
  110 Metaphysics
  120 Epistemology
  130 Parapsychology and Occultism
  140 Philosophical Schools of Thought
  150 Psychology
  160 Logic
  170 Ethics
  180 Ancient, Medieval, and Eastern Philosophy
  190 Modern Western Philosophy
- **200 Religion**
  200 Religion
  210 Philosophy and Theory of Religion
  220 The Bible
  230 Christianity and Christian Theology
  240 Christian Practice and Observance
  250 Christian Pastoral Practice and Religious Orders
  260 Christian organization, Social work, and Worship
  270 History of Christianity

280 Christian Denominations
290 Other Religions
- **300 Social Sciences**
300 Social Sciences, Sociology, and Anthropology
310 Statistics
320 Political Science
330 Economics
340 Law
350 Public Administration and Military Science
360 Social Problems and Social Services
370 Education
380 Commerce, Communications, and Transportation
390 Customs, Etiquette, and Folklore
- **400 Language**
400 Language
410 Linguistics
420 English and Old English Languages
430 German and Related Languages
440 French and Related Languages
450 Italian, Romanian, and Related Languages
460 Spanish and Portuguese Languages
470 Latin and Italic Languages
480 Classical and Modern Greek Languages
490 Other Languages
- **500 Science**
500 Science
510 Mathematics
520 Astronomy
530 Physics
540 Chemistry
550 Earth Science and Geology

560 Fossils and Prehistoric Life
570 Life Sciences; Biology
580 Plants (Botany)
590 Animals (Zoology)
- **600 Technology**
600 Technology
610 Medicine and Health
620 Engineering
630 Agriculture
640 Home and Family Management
650 Management and Public Relations
670 Manufacturing
680 Manufacture for Specific Uses
690 Building and Construction
- **700 Arts and Recreation**
700 Arts
710 Landscaping and Area Planning
720 Architecture
730 Sculpture, Ceramics, and Metalwork
740 Drawing and Decorative Arts
750 Painting
760 Graphic Arts
770 Photography and Computer Art
780 Music
790 Sports, Games, and Entertainment
- **800 Literature**
800 Literature, Rhetoric, and Criticism
810 American Literature in English
820 English and Old English Literatures
830 German and Related Literatures
840 French and Related Literatures

850 Italian, Romanian and Related Literatures
860 Spanish and Portuguese Literatures
870 Latin and Italic Literatures
880 Classical and Modern Greek Literatures
890 Other Literatures
- **900 History and Geography**
900 History
910 Geography and Travel
920 Biography and Genealogy
930 History of Ancient World (to ca. 499)
940 History of Europe
950 History of Asia
960 History of Africa
970 History of North America
980 History of South America
990 History of Other Areas

For more information visit:

https://www.oclc.org/content/dam/oclc/dewey/resources/summaries/deweysummaries.pdf

Universal Decimal Classification:

Main Tables (schedules). These first numbers in the classification indicate which class the item belongs in.

- 0 Science and Knowledge, Organization, Computer Science, Information Science, Documentation, Librarianship, Institutions and Publications
- 1 Philosophy and Psychology
- 2 Religion and Theology
- 3 Social Sciences
- 4 Vacant
- 5 Mathematics and Natural Sciences
- 6 Applied Sciences, Medicine and Technology
- 7 The Arts, Entertainment and Sport
- 8 Linguistics and Literature
- 9 Geography and History

For more information visit:

http://www.udcc.org/index.php/site/page?view=about_structure

Library of Congress Classification
Letters and titles of the main classes.

- A—General Works
- B—Philosophy, Psychology and Religion
- C—Auxiliary Sciences of History
- D—World History and History of Europe, Asia, Africa, Australia, New Zealand, etc.
- E—History of the Americas
- F—History of the Americas
- G—Geography, Anthropology, and Recreation
- H—Social Sciences
- J—Political Science
- K—Law
- L—Education
- M—Music and Books on Music
- N—Fine Arts
- P—Language and Literature
- Q—Science
- R—Medicine
- S—Agriculture
- T—Technology
- U—Military Science
- V—Naval Science
- Z—Bibliography, Library Science and Information Resources (general)

For more information visit:

https://www.loc.gov/catdir/cpso/lcco/

Other online resources:

American Library Association:

https://www.ala.org/

American Library Association, Library Bill of Rights:

https://www.ala.org/advocacy/intfreedom/librarybill

The Association for Rural and Small Libraries:

https://www.arsl.org/

Library of Congress

https://www.loc.gov/

OCLC Global Library Cooperative

https://www.oclc.org/en/home.html

Public Libraries Online:

http://publiclibrariesonline.org/

Nathan A. Hansen was nominated for the Lori Wallin Creative Writing Award in 2017. He served on the editorial board of the *Trestle Creek Review's* 2017 edition and the selection committee for the Northwest Undergraduate Conference in the Humanities in 2016. Nathan graduated from the Creative Writing and English program at Southern New Hampshire University. He now facilitates writer workshops, author presentations, and represents his library district on the North Idaho Literary Arts panel. He works as an information specialist, helping people locate hard-to-find and obscure resources through the library. His writing has been featured in the *Trestle Creek Review* and *Deep Wild Journal*.

Nathan spends his free time with his two kids, wife, and dog wandering through the mountains of north Idaho in all kinds of weather. He has hiked through 24 national parks and monuments; his favorite is Canyonlands in central Utah.

You can visit his website at nahansen.com.

www.ingramcontent.com/pod-product-compliance
Lightning Source LLC
Chambersburg PA
CBHW070913080526
44589CB00013B/1275